SANTO NINO, THE BODY of CHRIST

SANTO NINO, THE BODY of CHRIST

ROMITO S. OLAGUER

SANTO NINO, THE BODY OF CHRIST

All Scriptural Verses are taken from KJV, King James Version of the Holy Bible. *Unless otherwise indicated. Public Domain.*

Santo Nino, The Body of Christ
Romito S. Olaguer
For
Santo Nino Chapel of
Aromin, Echague, Isabela, Philippines
www.membersboc.com
e-mail: bombom.49@membersboc.com or
email: samaritanhp@yahoo.com
Copyrights registration for this book has been applied for, and 2 copies were sent to Library of Congress, Copyright Office – TX; Case / SR# 1-1569958331

iUniverse books may be ordered through booksellers or by contacting:

iUniverse
1663 Liberty Drive
Bloomington, IN 47403
www.iuniverse.com
1-800-Authors (1-800-288-4677)

Because of the dynamic nature of the Internet, any web addresses or links contained in this book may have changed since publication and may no longer be valid. The views expressed in this work are solely those of the author and do not necessarily reflect the views of the publisher, and the publisher hereby disclaims any responsibility for them.

Any people depicted in stock imagery provided by Thinkstock are models, and such images are being used for illustrative purposes only.
Certain stock imagery © Thinkstock.

ISBN: 978-1-4917-4678-3 (sc)
ISBN: 978-1-4917-4679-0 (e)

Printed in the United States of America.

iUniverse rev. date: 10/23/2014

Contents

In everything we pray; likewise, in every blessing we receive we share; also in everything give love to all for the reward is more than a trillion times everything you gave.

Jesus Christ gave everything he has at the Cross to save and sanctify all mankind.

- He is the truth that set us free
- He is the one True Vine
- He is the way
- He is the Life
- He is the Tree of Life
- He is the light of the world
- He is the ransom for our sins
- He is the Lamb of the World
- He is the Bread of Life
- He is the Living Water
- He is our salvation, our all in all
- He is every thing to all of us, without Him we are all nothing.

TO MY READERS: Do not believe everything I wrote here except the Bible verses, until you have validated it against the scriptures. Each believer will receive unique revelation from the Holy Spirit: separate from one another for as Members of the Body, we have different functions.

FOREWORD

The purpose for writing this book is to give all, I really mean all people around the world: who may have the privilege of reading it, a spiritual view of what the Kingdom of God is about. I hope this will open a window into the spirit world for all who wants to see what happens to their spirit and soul upon accepting Christ as their Lord Savior, and learn how the economy of God works. To those whose eyes and heart were opened by the Holy Spirit, it will be a fantastic experience. He will take us to new places and new heights. God guarantees it.

Only those who are called by the Father will know His words, and surely they will come to Christ. I also believe that those who have the appointed time to read, is called by the Father, for this book will lead them to become **Members of the Body of Christ.** Being in this Body nothing is impossible. We receive all the promises of God.

To write this book, I was led by the revelations from the Holy Spirit. He showed me, who is this image; the Image of the Holy Infant Jesus of Prague, the Santo Nino de Cebu, the Santo Nino de Atocha and the Mechlin Statue of Flanders, Belgium. Most Catholics will say He is the Baby Jesus. Why in the world Christ is a small boy again? Why Christ has not come back yet? That is the mystery. But the Holy Spirit revealed to me, why? And the Answers: You will find it here.

This book is dedicated to all of my brothers and sisters in the **Body of Christ** and to all who are called and who desired to be added as **Members.**

Repent and Rejoice for the Kingdom of God is at Hand, Our Final Destination.

The Christian Faith

I Bless Our Father in Heaven, Jesus Christ, The Holy Spirit, Virgin Mary and All the Saints. Likewise, blessings to All who may read this book, to all my neighbors and to all people in the four corners of this world that he or she may be called by our Father to become one of Christ' sheep or believer. **Let us call them by their names,** in the same manner as Jesus called Lazarus by name. So they may become Children of the God of Abraham, Isaac and Jacob. I pray in the Holy Name of Christ Jesus. Amen.

John 6:37 *All who the Father gives Me shall come to Me and him who comes to Me I will in no wise cast out.*

John 6:38 *For I come down from Heaven not to do My Own Will, but the Will of Him Who sent Me.*

John 6:65 *Therefore, said I unto you, that no one can come unto Me, except it were given unto him of my Father.*

"him who comes to Me." God declares that He calls all of mankind regardless of faith or race or situation to come to Him. To All:

whomsoever will repent of their sins and accept Jesus Christ as their Lord and Savior, and Son of Father God, he shall receive God's gift of grace and mercy and have eternal life.

Jesus invites us to have a **holy spiritual family relationship** with the Father, for we are spirit beings, created in His image and likeness destined to rule and reign with God. Otherwise He will not invite us this way. However, humans are the only spirit beings with a body of flesh, blood and bones.

John 6:47 *Verily, verily, I say unto you, He who believes in Me has Everlasting Life.* Eternal Life immediately (instantly) received upon "believing".

See Acts 16:31. *And they said,* (Paul and Silas) *Believe on the Lord Jesus Christ, and you shall be saved, and your house.* When fathers believe, we save our selves and also those who are members of our family.

God's Promises:
For the First Advent of the Messiah.

Isaiah 9:6 *For unto us a Child is born, unto us a Son is given: and the Government shall be upon His Shoulder: and His Name shall called Wonderful, Counselor, The Mighty God, The Everlasting Father, The Prince of Peace.* These are the names that Christ was and will be identified, His first coming.

- Wonderful – He is meek, kind, loving (unconditional love), gracious, and merciful. He gives us our daily bread.

- Counselor – His Gospel provides us great wisdom on how to live in this earth where we are virtually in the shadow and in the valley of death. His wisdom will guide us through the maze of evil traps, and finally leads us to **Membership in the Body of Christ**, where we attain victory, we desperately need.
- The Mighty God - He is all Powerful. He is our shield and Armor of God. He provides us protection and safety from the principalities of evil, 24/7/366. Christ guarantees us this protection as long us we abide in Him.
- The Everlasting Father – He is our only Father all through eternity. His attributes will never change He is the same yesterday, today and tomorrow. His promises, and covenants with our forefathers will live forever, as we are all, who are in Him.
- Prince of Peace – He is the only one who can bring us, sinners to commune and receive peace with the Holy Father. Rest and peace that passes all understanding.

Isaiah 9:7 *Of the increase of His Government and peace there shall be no end, upon the throne of David, and upon His Kingdom, to order it and to establish it with judgment and with justice from hencefort even forever. The zeal of the Lord of Host will perform this.* Once the gathering of the Body of Christ is complete then this prophecy is fulfilled.

Isaiah 9:8 *The Lord sent a word into Jacob, and it hath lighted upon Israel.* It is up to the Father to call as much believer or church to become **Members of the Body of Christ.** The Church can help hasten the calling of believers by praying for their friends and relatives by name that they may be included as **Member of**

the Body of Christ. It is the duty of the Church to obey Christ commandment, the Great Commission to bring and teach the Gospel to ends of the world.

In **Isaiah 9:6**: Obviously, the Prophet Isaiah has told this prophecy to the entire Israel that the Messiah is coming in the form of a Child. But it was not well understood, because when Jesus came, most of the Jews were clueless as to, who Jesus is, their Messiah. They know Him as the son of Joseph and Mary, and not much more.

Another Jewish belief is that, how can something great come out of Nazareth. It is a normal human apprehension, even today, if you come from the boondocks, nobody is going to give you much respect. I believe for these reasons why a very low percentage of people who hears the Gospel of Christ accepts, too many stumbling blocks in our spiritual environment.

What can we do to remove all the stumbling blocks? The answer is: **we pray, we start with the Lord's Prayer.**

Chapter 1

Believers' or Lords' Prayer

How to Pray:

Matt 6:5 *And when you pray, you shall not be as the hypocrites are; for they love to pray in the synagogues and in the corners of the streets, that they may be seen of men. Verily I say unto you. They have their reward.*

Matt. 6:6 *But you, when you pray, enter into your closet, and when you have shut your door, pray to your Father which sees in secret shall reward you openly.*

When traveling, the Jews uses the Tallit or prayer shawl to cover their heads when praying. This serves as a closet or secret place to pray. Jesus, being a Rabbi also used the Tallit.

Mark 5:25-34 Remember the woman who touched the hem of Jesus' garments? Some believed it was the wings (corner/hem) of the Tallit that she touched, that she received the healing from Jesus. But Jesus told the woman *"Daughter, thy faith hath made thee whole; go in peace, and be whole of thy plague"*. They believe there is power in the tallit. Obviously the power comes from the wearer, any one who is a man anointed by God. Also read **Matt. 9:20-22.**

Let us take a closer look at this miracle. It illustrates that although God can virtually do all things, He is showing us that miracles like these can only come to pass with our consciousness that we must participate with true Faith, focused solely on Christ and His finished work at the cross. Repeatedly, Jesus said; "I abide in you, and you abide in me."

To fulfill the Word of God, faith allows us to become **Members of the Body of Christ**. Of course, faith must be validated with works for us to bear fruit. Doing the work is not hard by virtue of faith. So:

Matt. 6:7 *But when you pray, use not vain repetition as the heathen do for they think that they shall be heard for their much speaking.*

Matt. 6:8 *Be not you therefore like unto them; for your Father* (Heavenly Father) *knows what things you have need of, before you ask Him.* Our Father will not deny us of when we ask for uncommon blessings: "knows what things you have need of" means provision of things that suits the will of God. Other than those of the will of Him, do not expect anything. Again, to be an insider to receive uncommon blessings, **Membership in the Body of Christ** is required.

Matt. 6:9 *After this manner therefore pray you: **Our Father Who is in Heaven, Hallowed be Your Name.*** We must bless God first, before God can hear our prayers. To bless God is an act of worship that we must not forget. The God who is in Heaven is the only true God. Jesus made sure of it that we are not worshipping other Gods.

Matt. 6:10 *Your Kingdom come, Your Will be done in Earth, as it is in Heaven,*

Matt. 6:11 *Give us this day our daily bread,*

Matt. 6:12 *And forgive us our debts, as we forgive our debtors.*

Matt. 6:13 *And lead us not into temptation, but deliver us from evil: Glory be to the Father, to the Son and to the Holy Spirit; For Yours is the kingdom, and the power, and the glory, forever. Amen.*

Supposedly, this is the model or template of our prayers when we pray. To ask for supplications for our daily needs as well as desires of our hearts. And to most of us is simply to enjoy life in this earth. Then we must pattern our prayers this way.

As for me, I will make substitution for verse # 11 to fit what I will ask from my Father. These petitions: can be for healing of bodily affliction or diseases; wisdom, spiritual afflictions like adultery, or the forgiveness of sin. To others it could be healing the extraordinary spiritual affliction of homosexuality, which I believe is way harder to deal with. For the person will believe it is the right thing to do because it feels right. (Sad thing is: when something feels right, usually it is so wrong). Or for extra financial needs; for romance and affairs of the heart; or for other needs outside of the ordinary. When asking for uncommon blessings to come to pass, we need to sow a seed. Go for 1000x fold seed. We should emulate King Solomon for he sacrificed 1000 Burnt Offering to the Lord. These are just a few examples. You can substitute anything that concerns you, especially whatever the desires of your heart that are good. We can expect for whatever we asked for to come to pass. Jesus said; anything you asked the Father in His name, He will do it.

"Give us our daily bread" can also mean a daily communion with our Lord Jesus, where we partake of the bread as His broken body as often as we can and to proclaim His death, until He comes again.

The rest of the prayer pattern I will keep as is. These verses I will not dare to change, because they are so important for my Spiritual Wellness. For they will surely lead me: to the **Body of Christ.** Read **Rom. 12, 1 Cor. 12:14-31**

Let us examine what the Believer's prayer means: We can only understand all these verses if we read through the Eyes of a Jewish Jesus, meaning we must put our hearts and mind in the holy spiritual dimension. This means we abide in Christ.

Verse 9 – We must bless, give reverence and venerate our Father in heaven; the Father of our Patriarch Abraham, Isaac and Jacob, our Jewish roots. When we pray, we must not forget; it is from them where our blessings flow; where our blessings/sustenance are coming from. Without their unfailing faith, we have nothing. We are the beneficiaries of their good works.

Verse 10- The Kingdom come is Jesus Christ in His first advent and the Will of the Father is instituted on Earth. Repent! The

Kingdom of God is at hand, that is the exhortation of John the Baptist.

In the **Gospel of Luke 17:21**, it says: *the Kingdom of God is amongst you*. Other version says; the Kingdom of God is within you. Pontius Pilate asked Jesus. Where is your kingdom? Jesus answered: My Kingdom is not of this world. John 18:36, Actually, I believe, it is also in this earth, but it is in the spiritual dimension and not in the flesh or mortal dimension. As people, we only look to things that our eyes can see. Expand your areas of perception. Read the Holy Bible through the eyes of a Jewish Jesus, and be amazed.

Verses 12 and 13: It is very important that we ask our Father of these things, because they (our debts and temptations) are our stumbling blocks. Jesus redeemed our debts by dying at the Cross. If Satan desires our soul, Jesus prays for us so that our faith will not fail us. God will not allow us unto temptation.

These stumbling blocks have to be removed, if not, we can't enter into the **Kingdom of God** and commune with Him, because the temptation and the deception in the natural world' laid out by Satan is strong. If sin remains in us we cannot partake of the bread of life laid out by Jesus even though God's grace is available, by Jesus' finished work at the Cross. Remove the stumbling blocks by accepting Jesus as your Lord and Savior.

Gal. 1:4 *Who gave himself for our sins, that He might deliver us from this present evil world, according to the will of Our God and Father.*

As partakers of the Bread of Life we become **Members of the Body of Christ.** (Read Rom 12). The breaking of the bread ritual

5

is also very important. We proclaim His death until He (Christ) comes the second time.

In summary: The Lord's or Believer's Prayer always leads us to the **Body of Christ**. So it is very important that we must use it, every time we want to communicate with our Lord Jesus. It is only through Him we get connected to our Father in Heaven. Thru faith, we affirm in prayer in this manner:

The Apostles' Creed (A Profession of Faith)

1. I believe in One God, the Father Almighty, Maker of Heaven and Earth, of all things visible and invisible.
2. I believe in one Lord Jesus Christ, the only begotten Son of Lord, born of the Father before all ages, God from God, Light from Light, true God from True God, begotten, not made, consubstantial with the Father; through Him all things were made. For us men and for our salvation he came down from Heaven, and became man,
3. And by the Holy Spirit was incarnate of the Virgin Mary, and became man.
4. For our sake he was crucified under Pontious Pilate; He suffered death and was buried: He descended into hell:
5. On the third day He rose again from the dead:
6. He ascended into Heaven, and sits at the right hand of God the Father Almighty:
7. From thence He shall come to judge the quick and the dead, and His Kingdom will have no end.
8. I believe in the Holy Ghost, the Lord, the giver of life, who proceeds from the Father and the Son, who with

the Father and the son is adored and glorified, who was spoken through the prophets.

9. I believe in the Holy Catholic Church: the communion of Saints:
10. The forgiveness of sins;
11. The resurrection of the body:
12. And the life everlasting. Amen.

This Apostles Creed is the summary of the Doctrine of the Four Gospel of our Lord Christ Jesus in the New Testament. Excerpts from: the Roman Misal, Third Edition. www.magnificat.com

The Nature of Christ

God is a giver. **Luke 11:9** *And I say unto you, Ask, and it shall be given you; seek, and you shall find; knock, and shall be opened unto you.*

Luke 11:10 *For every one who asks receives; and he who seeks finds; and to him who knocks it shall be opened.* The above 2 verses tells explicitly what kind of God we have. We have a very caring God. He tells us how to approach Him for our needs, whether they are spiritual or material in nature, because we need it both. Of course it must be within His will to expect a positive result. God's will for us, are written in the Scriptures. He has promised it to us, all we have to do is claim it.

Blessings:

Jer. 17:7 *Blessed is the man who trusts in the Lord, and whose hope the Lord is.*

Psalm 41:2 *The Lord will preserve him, and keep him alive, and he shall be blessed upon the earth: and you will not deliver him unto the will of his enemies.* The divine protection is bestowed to those who trust in the Lord.

These are God's promises: to those, who believes and loves Him. How can we be wrong if we are **Members of the Body of Christ?** We cannot, because we have His blessed assurance. The only place: where membership is guaranteed, with Divine Benefits.

A man is not a real Man if he does not abide in Christ, for he cannot be a High Priest without Christ abiding in him.

CHAPTER 2

The Great Invitation

Matt. 11:28 *COME UNTO ME, all you who labour and are heavy laden, and I will give you rest.*

Matt. 11:29 *Take My yoke upon you and learn of Me, for I am meek and lowly in heart: and ye shall find rest unto your souls.*

Matt. 11:30 *For my yoke is easy and My burden is light.*

What a promise by our Lord Jesus Christ. He requires very little from us, just have Faith, learn to seek and **have Trust in Him**. **"JUST COME UNTO ME"** We can never go wrong with this very re-assuring Invitation. For God, the Human Spirit is too important that He does not want to lose even one. He will seek every sheep that is Lost.

Heb. 10:22 *Let us draw near with a true heart with full assurance of Faith; having our hearts sprinkled from and evil conscience, and our bodies washed with pure water.* Christ is the only one who can make us holy by shedding His holy blood on the cross as ransom for our sins.

9

After Christ crucifixion: **The Free Gift of God is Grace and Mercy was now available to all men. That guarantees the Salvation of our Spirit and soul; by the Finished Work of Christ at the cross.**

By His stripes we are healed. All our Spiritual afflictions are no more.

What is the most important thing in Your Life?

A Career? Is it Money? A Home? Is it your Children? A Loving Wife, or Husband? A Car? All of these things and more combined will not suffice or matter much, though they are very important for us to live in this world. To enjoy all these things, we must first accept Jesus Christ' invitation "**Come Unto Me**" and Seek ye first the Kingdom of God, to secure a position **or Membership in the Body of Christ, the most important.** Matthew 6:33

Key: Acts 3:19 *Repent ye therefore; and be converted, that your sins may be blotted out when the times of refreshing shall come from the Presence of the Lord;*

Acts 3:20 *And He shall send Jesus Christ, which before was preached unto you.* Christ 2nd advent.

Acts 3:21 *Whom the Heaven must receive until the times of restitution of all things, which God has spoken by the mouth of all His Holy Prophets since the world began.* This is the Church Age or the Dispensation of Grace period. New Testament.

Repentance is an admission of guilt with humility by the sinner and that God is right and just, in asking man to ask for forgiveness of his sins. We must allow the Holy Spirit to work in us and be converted to the Gospel of Grace. And God will forgive anyone who asks and repent.

First and Foremost: Secure the Salvation of our true self: Our Spirit and Soul thru the gift of grace by our Lord Jesus Christ.

No Other God in the Universe:

Jesus Christ Revealed:

Isaiah 45:5 *I am the Lord,* **and there is none else,** *there is no God beside Me: I girded you, though you have not known Me.* Let us make no mistake about this, believe.

John the Baptist: Matt. 2:2 *And saying, Repent you: for the Kingdom of Heaven is at hand,*

Matt. 2:3 *For this is he who was spoken of the Prophet Isaiah, saying. The voice of the one crying in the wilderness;* **Prepare you the Way of the Lord, make His paths straight.** God's will for John, the Baptist, he cleared the path for Christ's Ministry.

Jer. 29:11 *For I know the Plans I have for you, declares the Lord, plans to Prosper you and not to harm you, plans to give you hope and a future.* NIV

Jer. 29:11 *For I know the thoughts that I think toward you, says the Lord, thoughts of peace, and not of evil, to give you an expected end.* KJV.

11

Please check out and analyze the above verses from two different translations from the original Greek manuscripts: The NIV verse seems to be more materially inclined than KJV verse. While the KJV verse is more spiritual.

To add perspective to the analysis; the KJV was translated word for word, while the NIV was translated by context. To the reader, make your call. There is no right or wrong answer.

If you have accepted Christ Jesus as your Lord and Savior in true faith: You become a **Member of the Body of Christ**. Then the Holy Spirit will speak to you, He will explain to you and will tell you, of the will of the Father, for as members we have different task to do. For your fulfillment of these tasks, you will bear fruit that will glorify the Father. For example: The Father's will for Jesus Christ is to redeem man from sin or man's affiliation and bondage to Satan. Christ was able to fulfill all of God's commandments to man as written in the Old Testament books. Up to the point that Christ has to shout while on the Cross: **Mark 15:34** *And at the ninth hour Jesus cried in a loud voice, saying, E- lo-i, El-lo-i, la-ma sa-bach-tha-ni? Which is, being interpreted, My God, My God, why hast thou forsaken me?* For Christ finishing His work at the Cross He became the First Fruits. Therefore be cognizant of what is the will of our Father for us. Then, just like Jesus we have to fulfill and also finish the work. We will also bear fruit. I know we will not duplicate Christ's work. The Father will not forsake us.

If we have questions, He will give us the most profound answers immediately. He will provide for our needs. After you have received Jesus' gift of Grace, there should be no turning back.

Give thanks and praise to the Lord, for He will amaze you until you finish the race.

Guide: The Holy Spirit will communicate with us in many forms and different ways: By dreams, visions, hearing His still small voice or by revelations, or by His presence or by events that we will experience. My feeling of the presence of the Holy Spirit is like a very warm embrace. And silently, I ask: Is it you Lord? And if we ask, we will receive an answer right away. This is what I have experienced. Just be cognizant of the Lords' messages. Then act on it. Our obedience is the key to receive His blessings. Since we bear fruit, our Father will not cut us off from the Vine.

So, when we finally face God, we are not coming empty handed, especially for the men. For the men must offer their body to God as a living sacrifice, holy and perfect. **Read 1 Cor. 11:3.**

As I checked the reality that so many people don't know much about the Truth of the God of Abraham, Isaac and Jacob. In my estimates only about 30% of the world's population have a fairly good understanding of the Gospel of Christ. What happens then to the 70%. Therefore there must be a very Big Problem

CHAPTER **3**

The Problem

In the first two chapters, I put into perspective, if all men accept the fact that there is a Holy and Loving God. And that He has sent His only begotten Son Jesus Christ to Earth, to redeem God's beloved creation man from sin (bondage to Satan). If we had obeyed God, then everything on this planet Earth will be pretty good. Knowing that God had unilaterally made covenant after covenant, promise after promise of prosperity and all the good things man will need to live in this Earth. Notice that God made all this promises to Abraham, Isaac, Jacob, Moses, King David and King Solomon. There is one thing in common with these men: They all loved God. We have a rich God. God did not create man to be poor, to live in discomfort and misery.

But why in reality, life is not pretty good to most of us? If only we understand the **Words of God** in the Holy Bible, our instruction manual, how to live on earth, I believe we will not have all these predicaments. How come most of us are suffering? So many people are living in poverty, it seems we live in a world of lack, where suffering is a common daily regimen. Estimates show, only about 30% of the worlds' population believes in the One True God, the God of Abraham, Isaac and Jacob. No wonder only about 30%, are well off.

But what about the remaining 70%, why don't they believe? I believe the Holy Bible has presented all its facts and figures so convincingly that anyone who read or heard about it will be convinced by the truth and be converted. Unfortunately the answer is no. The stumbling block is also great. So I searched for answers:

Q. Why would I need God? The following are common beliefs, sayings and alibis:

a) I have not seen god since I was a child and it is not taught in my school?

b) I did not commit a crime? I am good person.

c) My life is perfect; I am rich, and can buy everything I want. I don't need god.

d) A few of my friends don't like me sometimes, they say I am a pain in the neck, but that is ok even if I am little bit lonely. I can live with that. I don't need God's help.

f) Sometimes as if I am missing something, it bothers me, but I don't know what it is. Whatever?

g) Yes, I heard about god, but there are so many religions or faith, so many types of god. I don't know who, to believe? Which one will I choose? I am confused.

h) Some say; there is no god; it is only a pigment of man's imagination.

i) Some of my friends are ashamed to admit that they have a god. They don't want to talk about it.

j) Some says: I was not created. I know we evolved from apes and monkeys, and this is how we are taught in my school. I think I believe it because none of my classmates complains if it is true or not, so I just tag along.

The above beliefs and justifications are only a few, and you, the reader can think or encounter more and can add to the list.

Answer: I can say and this is what I believe: Satan has created all the confusion in this world to oppose God, as it is written. Even though Satan has something to do about man's tribulation, I cannot completely blame him, for man's sin is only half his fault. Man owns the other half. My advice to all: by all means do not conform to evil ideas. Reject the works of Evil by all means, and accept what God promised us. Continue reading for more wisdom.

Psalm 14:1 *The fool hath said in his heart. There is no God. They are corrupt, they have done abominable works, there is none that doeth good.*

In today's world: half of man's Greatest Problem is his Unbelief in a True God. The result is rebellion. Made worse by denial and hardening of the hearts to willfully and knowingly oppose God. The other half is the work of the devil.

I cannot blame Adam and Eve much, for the sin was accounted unto men, they did not have a written Bible yet as a guide. They have not experienced the consequences of dying in the spirit.

How about us, people of the present time? Until now, we still don't realize, that we have a dead spirit to take care of aside

from our living body and soul. We already know that Adam and Eve died, and all those who did not accept the free gift of Grace by God.

My Question? Why do we still follow their footsteps in sin? Is our generation still so dumb that we still don't know who we are? And make the same mistakes over and over again, that some people calls it insanity. I guess we are insane, indeed. **On top of our insanity,** we knowingly spend millions of dollars in medical care for our flesh and bones. Which we give so much priority when we know will ultimately die anyway. But we do not want to spend nothing for the wellness of our spirit; which is who we really are? We are created first by God in the spirit. Then He formed us in the flesh. We are worth so much more important than anything else in this world. He created us in His image, and in His Likeness and we are the apple of His eyes. God's plan is to love us no matter what. Why do we still oppose Him? Are we scared of God? To my potential brothers and sisters, please come to Christ. He is meek and kind. He came to save us all, if all will accept.

Because of man's weakness: We were tempted, deceived and ultimately, we committed SIN. And once we are separated from our Creator God, our problems abounded for we are virtually on our own to fend for ourselves. We suffer until now. We also know we have a Redeemer, but we still take Jesus Christ for granted, even if we know He is the only solution. We still want it our way. **Why?**

God said: *Man does not live by bread alone, but from every word that proceeds from the mouth of God.* **Deut. 8:3**

Another thing: If man doesn't have a spirit, why would Jesus Christ come and bother to suffer for our sins at the Cross of Calvary? **Look up, young man look up! Think about it!**

My advice to unbelievers:

Prov. 3:5 *Trust in the Lord with all your heart; and lean not unto your own understanding.* Humble yourselves and learn the Words of God and have Faith to be transformed into a new creation. Ready to be molded by God to do His will. There is a Spiritual Life in every one of us that will continue on to live, even after the death of flesh and bones. What will be your choice: Eternal life or 2nd Death? If you are still in doubt, it is better to check it out. Give Christ a chance to live in your hearts. You will never be sorry. This I guarantee, because Christ has guaranteed.

Prov. 3:6 *In all your ways acknowledge Him, and He shall direct your ways.* In this worldly life, we cannot survive on our own, the principalities of evil is way too strong for us to overcome alone. We need God's help in every which way we go. This way we keep accidents from happening in our home, in our workplace and to places we go. Read Chapter 25 of this book.

We must acknowledge we are SINNERS:

Every man that ever lived this earth is a SINNER, except Jesus Christ. When man had disobeyed God's commandment not to eat of the fruit of the Tree of Knowledge of Good and Evil, for they will surely die we committed sin. And man died in his Spirit, Adam knew it, and eventually he died in the flesh later, but most of us in the next generation, does not know it or simply we do not want to acknowledge until now.

See Rom. 3:23 *For all have sinned, and come short of the Glory of God.*

Rom. 6:23 *For the wages of sin is death;* **but the gift of God is Eternal Life through Jesus Christ our Lord.**

1 John 1:8 *If we say we have no sin, we deceive ourselves, and the Truth is not in us.* Now that we know we are sinners, we must accept Christ as our Lord and Savior so that we also become holy and be counted as **Member of the Body of Christ.**

For God, the Human Spirit is too much to waste.

The First Adam, Started The Problem

Rom. 5:12 *Wherefore, as by one man sin entered into the world* (thru Adam), *and death by sin passed upon all men for that all have sinned:* All have sinned because of Adam's acceptance of the temptation and the sin nature of Satan is now present in man. Satan is the author of sin. God will not look at sin.

Rom. 5:13 *For until the Law (Law of Moses) sin was in the world: but sin was not imputed when there is no Law.* Although sin abounds in the world, as then Satan rules the world, sin was not accounted to man yet until the Law of Moses was instituted. The Law was not designed by God to save man from bondage to evil rather it was to inform man, that man is a sinner. And sin has to be dealt with by the Blood of Jesus, for it is the only way to atone for man's sin and be declared sinless again.

Rom. 5:14 *Nevertheless death reigned from Adam to Moses, even over them who had not sinned after the similitude of Adam's transgression, who is the figure of Him Who was to come.* Even to those who have not sinned per se, but every one has the sin nature, **the seed of Satan was impregnated in man.** No one will be born without it, **except for one man named Jesus Christ, who was conceived by the Holy Spirit, "the figure of Him who is to come."**

The Second Adam, The Solution

Apostle Paul illustrates the Contrast between the two Adams'. The first Adam was created and the Second Adam was begotten.

Rom. 5:15 *But not as the offence, so also is the free gift. For if through the offence of one many be dead, much more the grace of God, and the gift by Grace, which is by one man, Jesus Christ, has abounded unto many.* Once again the Finished Work of Christ at the Cross, is magnified in these verse. Christ defeated death or Satan by His shed blood at Calvary and His resurrection. Thus making it possible for God's gift of Grace for those who will accept Christ and be justified by faith. The more offence, the more is the gift of Grace.

Rom. 5:16 *And not as it was by one man who sinned, so is the Gift for the judgment was by one to condemnation, but the Free Gift is of many offences unto Justification.* The first Adam's fall pushed man to condemnation but the Free Gift of Grace by the Love of Christ afforded man, Justification by Faith.

Rom. 5:17 *For if by one man's offence death reigned by one; much more they, which receive abundance of Grace and of the gift of Righteousness shall reign in Life by One, Jesus Christ.* By virtue of the Finished Work of Christ at the cross, the "abundance of grace" was made possible. What then will our choice be: God's Grace or wrath of God?

Rom. 5:18 *Therefore as by the offence of one judgment came upon all men to condemnation; even so by the Righteousness of One (Jesus Christ) the free gift came upon all men unto Justification of Life.* I pray that all who heard about Christ will accept Him, and that He is the only solution to remove all our sin, and our predicaments of being in condemnation to death, for He takes away our bondage to evil. **Obtaining Salvation Through Jesus Christ is the Most important and only Solution!** Because all Blessings flow through Him and to us, we receive.

Rom. 3:24 ***Being Justified freely, by His Grace through the Redemption that is in Christ Jesus.*** What more can we ask for? Sadly, most people take this privilege for granted. We put our own true self, our spirit, always in peril. Even though we know it is bound for eternal suffering. **Rather we must put our selves bound for greatness, through our Lord Jesus.**

1 John 1:8 *If we say that we have no sin, we deceive ourselves, and the Truth is not in us.* We lied and are only fooling our selves.

1 John 1:9 *If we confess our sins, He is faithful and just to forgive us our sins, and to cleanse us from all unrighteousness.* Nothing else makes it clearer than this. Jesus is the Truth. We are not only forgiven but also clothe in righteousness, worthy to commune with God.

21

CHAPTER 4

In the Beginning

Earth: The Source, Father God.

First and Foremost: When it comes to matters of faith: All must come to terms and deal with the Holy Book, called the Bible that starts in **Old Testament**:

Gen. 1:1 *In the beginning, God created the Heavens and **the Earth.*** God knows in advance that writing the Bible, someone will do every means to discredit God of His deity and try to obliterate His Words, and for God to remove any doubts and confusion once and for all, God has declared that He is the Creator; because any other forms of faith or religion or beliefs or dogma that comes after, will be of no effect, for they are only imitation or copy, or heresy. Be aware for there is much worse, they are forms of idolatry and deception that distorts spiritual facts. It will represent no value to either God or man. All idolatry and deception is of Satan. He is our enemy no. 1.

The Bible's Authenticity Validated

To many atheist, unbelievers, the wicked and naysayers who says that the Bible is not relevant and true anymore in this day and age, simply because it was written more than 2000 years ago, are **dead wrong**.

The Bible says otherwise, the Living one True God is the same yesterday, today and tomorrow. He cannot change. **GOD IS NOT CONSTRAINED BY TIME.**

To the doubters of the Holy Bible, here are a few scriptural verses to prove that this book was not a product of fables and wishful thinking of man. Why do we believe anyone who says that the Scriptures are not true anymore because it is more than 2000 years old? Does God change or can we change that is spiritual in origin? We don't have that power. To prove to All that the Holy Bible is very, very, very True. And there should be no doubt. Here are 3 Scriptural verses to articulate the authenticity of the Holy Bible.

1) **2 Peter 1:16** *For we have not followed cunningly devised fables, when we made unto you the Power and Coming of our Lord Jesus Christ, but were eyewitnesses of His Majesty.* In the Transfiguration of Christ, Moses and Elijah, Matt 16:27-28. Peter was an eyewitness of this event

2 Peter 1:17 *For He received from God the Father Honor and Glory, when there came such a Voice to Him from the excellent Glory, This is my beloved Son, in whom I am well pleased.* This is an eyewitness account that was heard by many: Jesus being baptized with water, by John the Baptist in the river Jordan. This event is to usher in the Ministry of Christ. In the same manner, when we come to Christ we are also baptized by the Holy Spirit to sanctify our spirit, so that we are worthy to be **Members of the body of Christ**. Otherwise we cannot perform the will of the Father in Heaven.

2 Peter 1:18 *And this voice, which came from Heaven we heard, when we were with Him in the Holy Mount.* Therefore we must not dispute this claims. Another reason to believe what the Bible proclaims.

2 Peter 1:19 *We have a more sure Word of Prophecy; where unto you do well that you take heed, as unto a light that shines in a dark place, until the day dawn, and the Day Star arise in your hearts:* Christ is the Day Star, shining so bright. If we are in Christ we will shine as He is.

2 Peter 1:20 *Knowing this first that no Prophecy of the Scripture is of any private interpretation.* The Holy Spirit has declared that it is a fact that the Word of God did not come from the minds of Man.

2 Peter 1:21 *For the Prophecy came not in old time by the will of man; but Holy men of God spoke as they were moved by the Holy Spirit.* This explains the manner how the Word of God was written and given to mankind, by the Holy Spirit, which we can say without reservation, is the author of the Holy Bible.

2) **Benediction: Rom. 16:25** *Now to Him Who is of power to establish you according to my Gospel; and the Preaching of Jesus Christ, according to the Revelation of the Mystery, which was kept secret since the world began.*

Rom. 16:26 *But now is made manifest; and by the Scriptures of the Prophets, according to the Commandment of the Everlasting God, made known to all nations for the Obedience of Faith.* Faith in Christ guarantees our Salvation.

Rom. 16:27 *To God only wise, be Glory through Jesus Christ.* This proclaims that, the Gospel of Jesus Christ, was written by the Old Testament Prophets, now it came to pass and now made known to all nations for the Obedience by Faith. This leaves man no reason to doubt, but believe God's words for they are very, very true to the first degree. The Word of God is most profitable and nothing else.

If man does not believe, he is virtually on his own. Yes, man can find his way back to God, only with God's help, because somebody called him by name.

Matt. 26:53, *Thinkest, thou that I cannot now pray to my Father, and He shall presently give me more than twelve legions of Angels?* A validation that Christ came down from Heaven: because He can ask of anything from our Father. This is proof that: there is a holy relationship between Father and Son, as two person in the Godhead. As for man, he can also have the same degree of intimacy with the Father if we accept the Son. The word Trinity describes the relationship between the 3 person of the Godhead.

Matt. 26:54 *But how then shall the Scriptures be fulfilled, that thus it must be?* The scriptures is from God, thereby it will be fulfilled.

Matt. 26:56 *But all this was done, that the Scriptures of the Prophets might be fulfilled. Then all the Disciples forsook Him, and fled.*

Through the foreknowledge of the Holy Spirit predicted all these, many centuries in advance. It must be affirmed, the Holy Bible was written by Divine Inspiration to the men who wrote it and thus fulfilled. Man cannot do anything to stop the fulfillment of the Scriptures.

To Further Validate The Scriptures:

2 Tim. 3:14 *But you continue in the things which you have been assured of, knowing of whom you have learned them.* We have God's blessed assurance in our Faith.

2 Tim 3:15 *And that from a child you have known the Holy Scriptures, which are able to make you wise unto Salvation through Faith which is in Christ Jesus.*

The Word of God always points to Jesus Christ and what He did at Calvary. Christ's Finished Work.

2 Tim. 3:16 *All Scriptures is given* **by Inspiration of God, and is profitable for Doctrine, for reproof, for correction, for instruction in Righteousness.**

2 Tim. 3:17 *That the man of God may be perfect, thoroughly furnished unto all good works.* By virtue of the holiness of Scriptures, a man of God is made perfect through the Saving Grace of Christ: which was fulfilled by His Finished Work at the Cross. Without the cross as the means, man cannot secure Salvation even by Faith. Christ hanging on the Cross is proof that the sin debt of man was fully paid for. It is also proof that The Tree of Life and the Tree of Knowledge of Good and Evil were also reconciled at Calvary. Jesus was lifted up. Giving man freedom from Satan thru Faith.

Isaiah 42:5 *Thus saith God the Lord, He that created the heavens, and stretch them out, He that spread forth the earth, and that which cometh out of it; He that giveth breath unto the people upon it, and spirit that walk therein.* Our Father God is reminding all of His people, that He is the Supreme Being, who created all these things that man can see. The vastness, and grandeur of His creation is stretch out to the heavens; that no other can.

Added Notes: Satan is still trying to nullify the payment for man's sin, up to this day of the Church Age, by the teachings of Jehovah Witnesses doctrine that there was no Crucifixion of Christ that ever happened at Calvary. They say that it was just a straight vertical pole, and no horizontal member. They asked: where is it written in the Holy Bible that says it was a Cross, I say it is found in the book of Romans and the 4 Gospel books. I don't want to name names; but this account of deception, I can't let go, un-rebuked.

We can't continue to deceive our fellow men, with false Doctrine, I don't want to see my brothers and sisters ending up in Hell. To deceive your brothers is a grave sin. It is corruption of the facts.

The Holy Bible, a Spiritual Book

a) Humans are a spiritual being.
b) The Holy Bible is the only book that validates itself even for the thousands of years in its existence that we know of it. As a matter of fact it has not contradicted itself in

      its contents, not once. It is proof that it says what it says and that it is from God.

c) It is the Holy Spirit who wrote the Holy Bible through the Prophets. In it, He is showing us not only a peek or a glimpse of the spiritual dimension, but how the economy of God works. Actually the Bible is very spiritual in its context, translated on how to live a spiritual life in this world, which is in the valley of the shadow of death.

Yes, we live in a world surrounded by evil spirits. The Word of God serves as our guide to navigate the maze of evil traps set forth by Satan. In order to finish the race, our faith must be focused only on the finished work Christ at the cross. Therefore to live a spiritual life in this world: Believe, to be grafted as **Members of the Body of Christ**. Then we have the blessed assurance of salvation from sin, we are a 100 fold Church. God blessed us with unlimited unconditional love for Him, as we become a blessing to love our fellow man.

Let us give man a second chance:

Unbelief is man's first Sin. I believe, man cannot see the spiritual aspect of his life in this planet Earth anymore. Sure he can feel the presence of wind or air. He knows he is made of flesh, blood and bones. He also has a few wisdom, acquired knowledge through science and technology. With these, man believes he is already fully equipped, and does not need divine help. It is one of the main reasons, so many of us humans do not want to believe, that there is a Supreme Being, we call God, our Creator. Man is much more concerned of what he sees with his two eyes, but his eyes;

only fools him. Most of man's decisions are solely evaluated by using his 5 senses.

Therefore the idea of God is left out, and now we become a Godless society. No wonder our nation is plagued with problems.

It is time for man to use his 6th sense, get out of his box: the mortal dimension and reach out to the spiritual dimension (spiritual sense), explore it with God. And feel and know, there is a God, The Creator.

Another belief that is floating around, is that, if we can only practice the attitude of being good, being kind and does not treat other people wrong, that they already have earned a way to eternal life, or a way to God. **This is very far from the truth**. Though it sounds noble and right. People will ask why? What is wrong with this mind set? Too many wrong is going on. Just take a look at this world now, there are too much mayhem. The Bible says that to be declared saved, we must be **Member of the Body of Christ**. Just being declared good by our fellow men does not cut it.

And yet, another belief, that all world religion are worshiping the same god, **not so my friend**. There is only one God, a Godhead, represented in 3 person: **The Father, the Son (Jesus Christ-body) and the Holy Spirit as the God of Abraham, Isaac, and Jacob: Our Jewish Roots, The Judeo-Christian faith.**

Therefore, is it Ok to believe and worship other gods? **Absolutely NO**. Not The Way. The **problem** is, all these other beliefs cannot compare, they do not address the fact that man has the sin nature brought by the fall of Adam from grace. All men are sinners.

And all these other so called religion or faith does not have any comprehensive process in place for the redemption of sin and **provide salvation** (being free from bondage with Satan). It is up to man to work to save him. Whereas in the Judeo-Christian faith: salvation is laid out in a very comprehensive manner. The debt/sin of man is fully paid for; by the shed blood of Christ. That: by man's faith in Christ, man is redeemed. Christ said: I am THE Way, the Truth and the Life. This is the reason the Scriptures says the way to salvation or eternal life is narrow (only one way) but the way to perdition is broad for there are many ways to death (many religion).

In other faith: what their gods are requiring mainly in their so-called holy book: is the submission of man to commands and demands by their religious leaders and nothing really tangible in return for the follower. Only the leaders reap the benefits.

One Example; in Islam, the defining moment of their lives is to be suicide bombers or martyrs in the name of allah and call it jihad. What is the reward? It says the martyr will be given 70 virgins as a reward, ok. I guess, the promise of having sex with that many virgins is worth it, But why need to kill so many people? It does not say of eternal sex. What else? What kind of reward is that? Does man still be able to perform sex while they are in the spirit? I don't believe so. Man can do it only while in the flesh. The scripture does not say about begotten spirits. Sex is only for beings while in the flesh. Animals can perform sex. Sexual activity is the method of pro creation accorded to the animal kingdom.

What about female martyrs, what will they receive from allah? Is allah a good God? I don't believe so. The Koran does not say anything. There is no such thing as male virgins? Right? The word virgin should only be applied to describe to female humans who has not known any man. In here, we can see, that this doctrine is flawed. Still, almost half of the worlds' population believes, without really thinking. Then they call Islam a religion of peace? It is an obvious deception that most of us don't realize.

And they believed? Are you serious? How dumb can man be? Not knowing, that they believe in an unfair god with a set of unfair rules. If you fall for this type of doctrine, you are not a thinking man. You will be deceived by any small time conman anywhere.

Truth is, there is no other True God, but God of the Judeo-Christian Faith.

Let the Holy Spirit guide us, He will take us to Holy places man has never been.

Life and death exist for real. Both are eternal in the spiritual dimension. There is joy in the eternal life and suffering in the eternal death; which is spent in the Lake of Fire. What would you prefer? Our second chance to escape a certain death is no other than to be in Christ. We must abide in Him and allow our bodies to be His Temple.

Rev. 21:7 *He who overcomes shall inherit all things* (His faith is focused exclusively in the finished work of Christ at the Cross) *and I will be His God, and he shall be my son.*

Rev. 21:8 *But the fearful and unbelieving, and the abominable, and murderers, and whoremongers, and sorcerers, and idolaters, and* *all liars shall have their part in the lake, which burns with fire and brimstone, which is the second death.* It proclaims: that, this is the destiny of those who rejects Christ as Lord and Savior. Would you want to be there?

Knowing where man is going after his first death, i.e. death in our flesh; is the most important knowledge that we must have, that we are going to Paradise.

Our choice must be that we chose God, the Father through His Son, His only Begotten Son Jesus Christ. That man must not suffer the second death, which is separation from God.

Billion $ Question

Is there a God? Do man has a spirit just like God, created by Him, **yes.** Man is a spiritual being.

Gen. 1:26 *And God said, Let Us make man in Our image, after Our Likeness: and let them have dominion over the fish of the sea and over the fowl of the air, and over the cattle, and over all the earth, and over every creeping thing that creeps upon the earth.*

Gen. 1:27 *So God created man in His Own Image, in the Image of God created He him, male and female created He them.*

Gen. 1:28 *And God Bless them, and God said unto them, Be fruitful and multiply, and replenish the Earth, and subdue it and have dominion over the fowl of the air, and over every living thing that moves upon the Earth.*

Here, the "male and female created He them" is that, the spirit and soul of man without sin created in God's image, and in the Likeness of the spirit as God's. This is the real man and woman in the spirit and soul, capable of living the eternal spirit and soul, alive on this earth. In this instance, man has no flesh or form yet until verse; **Gen. 2:7** *And the LORD God formed man of the dust of the ground and breathed into his nostrils the breath of life and man became a living soul.* (Pertains to the soul and spirit of man.) God (He, Jesus) formed the clay in His image and Likeness and breathed into his nostrils. Therefore man (Adam) looks like God, not only in spirit but also in form, inside and out. If Adam's body is composed of cells, there is no doubt in my mind that the form or Body of Christ is also composed of cells, mortal and spiritual, that is.

And then, man was formed with flesh and blood; Adam was created. He has dominion over all the Earth. Man was God's friend and very precious to Him. Man is the apple of God's eyes. When God finished His creation, He said, it was good (holy). God has created man to live FOREVER with Him. First 2 chapters of the Bible, man is living without Sin and he is with God.

Also the last 2 Chapters of the Bible, man is again without sin. Man is finally sanctified to commune with his Maker again.

Complete Parallel: Three Dimensions

The Godhead is one; in three person. Tri unified. The Father, The Son and The Holy Ghost (spirit) are one. In layman's term; is called the Trinity. Man is also a three parts being; the human spirit (male and female), soul, and body/flesh are one. Proof that God created man in His own Image and Likeness. Only in the creation of man; that there is likeness with the Creator. Check out the previous page: **Gen. 1:26-28. It** is only in the human specie that God created a female spirit.

Notes: So many Bible scholars are saying that the word Trinity is not in the Bible and it is not valid to use it biblically. Just because it is not, it does not mean it is not correct to describe the Godhead as such. Unlike using the Biblical word "marriage" to describe union of homosexual is wrong, for it does not fit same sex union. Therefore, it must not be used by all means. Read **Deut. 29:29.**

How about: Angels (holy or unholy) are 1-part spirit beings and are males only and cannot procreate. God created the angels individually. And the animals too: are 1-part beings; one dimension. Once they die they are dead. There is no such thing as reincarnation of animals to another form of animal. No Biblical validation. Therefore a religious doctrine that promotes reincarnation is flawed.

We will take a break: A quote while watching Joel Osteen, Pastor of Lakewood Church, Houston, TX joked; *"A scientist tried to challenge God on how to make man; God said Ok and accepts, and the scientist vowed down and grabbed a bucketful of clay. God said oops, wait a minute, and told the scientist; Go, get your own dirt: That dirt is mine".* It is very, very funny.

The Two Trees

In the Garden of Eden, Gen. 2:8 *And the Lord God planted a Garden Eastward of Eden; and there He put the man whom He had formed.*

Gen. 2:9 *And out of the ground made the Lord God to grow every tree that is pleasant to the sight, and good for food; The Tree of Life.*

Jesus Christ, portrays the Tree Life, alive, in communion with God the Father forever. Meanwhile, the cross portrays the Tree of Knowledge of good and evil. It portrays human sufferings, pain and troubles, which is caused by evil spirit. The obvious reason why Adam was prohibited to eat of that tree because evil or Satan was also on that tree. And Satan corrupted the well being of Adam. Once Adam was corrupted, he lost his privileges to commune with God in Paradise. God could have given Adam a chance to come back only if Adam admitted his sin. Instead he chose to blame Eve and Eve blamed the serpent. A lesson is learned here: If we make a mistake, we must own it. Blaming others will make situation worse and leads to nothing or more loss spiritually. Material loss is not that important.

When Christ came, the will of the Father for Him is to redeem man from bondage to sin. So while hanging on the **cross, Christ has to die to reconcile man back to the Father.** Christ will make everything He touches, Holy.

In the same way that He touches our lives that He makes us holy. We are then sanctified by His blood, holy and perfect again in the eyes of the Father, ready and willing to do His will.

Read **Rev 2:7; 22:2;** And the Bread of Life; **John 6:48, 51**; To continue **Gen. 2:9** . . . *also in the midst of the Garden, and the Tree of Knowledge of Good and Evil.* Lucifer, Ex-Satan, portrays death, no hope, destined for the Lake of Fire and separated from God for rebellion. I believe the Lake of Fire will be the sun or just like it.

The two Trees represent man's choices: Life or Death. Free will given and respected by God.

In the New Testament:

John 1:1 *In the Beginning was the Word, and the Word was with God, and the Word was God.*

John 1:2 *The same was in the beginning with God.*

John 1:3 *All things were made by Him; and without Him; and without Him was not anything made that was made.* There will be no Universe without Christ.

John 1:4 *In Him was life; and the Life is Light of men.* Anyone who has Christ in him is holy.

John 1:5 *And the Light shines in darkness; and the darkness comprehended it not.* Satan represents darkness. The question is? What do we profit from darkness? We must ask ourselves this question and make a list.

John 1:1-5 above: The Holy Spirit proclaims the Deity of Jesus Christ. That He is the Great I AM of the Old and New Testament. Further proclaims He is God. He is the same yesterday, today and tomorrow.

CHAPTER 5

The First Commandment

This is God's first Commandment to Adam. **Gen. 2:16** *And the Lord God commanded the man. Saying; Of every tree of the Garden you shall freely eat;*

Gen. 2:17 *But of the Tree of Knowledge of Good and Evil, you shall not eat of it; for in the day that you eat thereof you shall surely die.* Even unto this present day, around 2000 years after Jesus Christ was Crucified at Calvary, at the Feast of the Passover; still almost three fourths of the world's population do not believe. This commandment is pretty much misunderstood. Adam died 930 years later after eating the forbidden fruit.

I believe, simply because we see and feel alive in the present condition of our flesh and bones, that there is nothing wrong with man's total wellbeing; but, in truth, man's spirit is dead. When the spirit is dead, mans' whole being: the soul and the flesh are also dead, though we appear to be alive. But what we don't realize is that we are separated from our God. After Adam's fall from God's grace, man's suffering started to abound, chaos, confusion, sickness, war among group of people and all sort of problems. Still man does not realize the real cause was that we are under evil influence and to make things worse, we do not heed the Word of God. If we listen to God, we can make our life better with less difficulties.

And much worse we blame God, why does He let all these bad things happen? Even to good people as we always say. Why, Why, Why? Man as always in all its generation, will not want find fault in self. I say it is man's abuse of the free will.

Man's Big Mistake

With this first commandment, disobedience is man's greatest fault though we can say that God has put man on probation period, but on the other hand, it was essential to man's spiritual development. Before the fall of man, he was higher in rank than the Satan. Adam's number was 6, just 1 below the complete number of God, which is 7. The number of the Satan then was 5. The number of the beast, big and small, is 4, why they stand and walk on four legs. But now it is reversed. The number 666 refers to Satan, not man.

The Image of Evil Spirits

Satan (ex-Lucifer) possessed the body of the serpent, so he can deal with Adam and Eve. And his demons (bad spirits and emissaries of evil), big and small, all looks like beast, some with horns and some none, some with tails and some none (described in the Book of Revelation and Daniel). Most are hairy. Bible calls them, graven images, for they are dead as far as God is concerned, because they too disobeyed God.

I believe one reason God said, "Jacob I love and Issau I hate. Why is Issau hairy?

Demon spirits can possess man, animals and critters. Example: The water buffalo, also called carabao is one of the favorite host for evil spirits other than man maybe because it is black. Water buffaloes are considered the best Beast of Burden because they are very strong, easy to train and tame. Thus forge a good working relationship with man. In the Asian tropical countries of Thailand, Burma, Vietnam and Philippines, during the monsoon season, many men are hit by lightning and die, by just being adjacent to this beast. The beast survives most of the time. Many people in that region are asking, why?

The scientific laws of lightning strikes, is often violated by this phenomenon and is not understood.

But if we put it in spiritual perspective, we might have an answer. Only God can create lightning. Demon Spirits are God's creation as well, that dwells beneath the Earth. So when evil spirit fails to completely hide beneath the Earth, they are hit by lightning strikes as punishment from God for their disobedience and transgressions. The evil spirit suffers but they don't die. When they are hit, they get thrown into far away places and will take days to come back to their assigned location. They are hurt and badly bruised.

Their suffering is eternal as well as human spirits who failed to accept the Saving Grace of Christ while man is still in the body, and has all the chance to be saved and not suffer. The human body is not designed to suffer pain, for man was created to commune with God. Therefore we must be scared to be away from God's protective realm, which is the Body of Christ. We receive this only by Faith.

Ishmael and Issau.

Issau is the first born of Isaac. And Ishmael is the first born of Abraham. Both were not anointed, but both are sons of God anointed men. Two things they have in common. Why both are not anointed?

The Bible did not tell us, why? What is the problem? God must have a pretty good reason. What do you think?

A man possessed by evil spirit: **Read Mark 5:2-20.**

The Wicked are Judged

Jer. 15:11 *The LORD said, verily it shall be well with your Remnant: verily I will cause the enemy to intreat you well in the time of evil and in time of affliction.* The Remnants are those who obeyed the Lord and will be spared from judgment and they will be mightily blessed.

In this verse the Lord will give the riches of the enemy or wicked to the holy remnants. An example of this; was when the Jews left Egypt in the time of Moses. The Lord required the Egyptians to pay the Jews 7 times the gold and silver for being enslaved for almost 4 centuries. These are still true in this Church Age.

Please be observant of the times and you will recognize the events that are happening in front of our very eyes. The riches of the wicked will be transferred to Churches of God.

Jer. 15:13 *Your substance and your treasures will I give to the spoil without price, and that for all your sins, even in all your borders.* The riches accumulated by the wicked will be taken away without a price. Why? These riches were stolen from the righteous (who worked hard). God promised that vengeance is His.

Jer. 15:14 *And I will make you pass with your enemies into a land, which you know not: for a fire is kindled in My anger, which shall burn upon you.* Aside from making the wicked recompense the righteous for lost wages, they will still be put in the Lake of Fire to suffer forever. My brothers and my friends; there is absolutely no incentive to be wicked.

Employers who are always riding on the backs of poor workers and paying very low wages: Beware for you are corrupting the system and taking advantage of the less fortunate. Just for a dollar more? Karma will surely fall on you. God says: vengeance is mine.

The Wicked and Unfaithful Rebuked

God's Warnings: **Isaiah 57:3** *But draw near hither, you sons of sorceress, the seed of the adulterer and the whore.* The Prophet is asking or inviting the wicked and the unfaithful in his days to repent and heed the Words of God instead of following other faith with no assurance or hope for Salvation from bondage to Satan.

If the wicked remains in Spiritual adultery, meaning: believing in Gods other than the Judeo-Christians', there is no hope in them, in gaining **Membership in the Body of Christ.**

Isaiah 57:4 *Against whom do you sport yourself? against whom do you make a wide mouth, and draw out the tongue? Are you not children of transgression, a seed of falsehood.* The wicked has no right to discredit the good works of the righteous, for its fruits are coming from the Father.

CHAPTER 6

The Fall of Man

Why man committed SIN? Gen. 3:2, *And the woman said unto the serpent. We may eat of the fruit of the trees of the Garden.*

Gen. 3:3 *But of the fruit of the tree which is the midst of the Garden, God has said, You shall not eat of it, neither shall you touch it, lest you die,*

Gen. 3:4 *And the serpent said unto the woman, You shall not surely die.*

Satan's Lie

Gen. 3:5 *For God does know that in the day you eat thereof, then your eyes shall be opened, and you shall be as gods, knowing good and evil.* Eve bought the lie. Satan will always present himself as something or someone else. I am a skeptic by all means. If we don't know how to validate his actions by the Word of God, then we are always free game for him. It is important that before we act on something that we might believe is from God, we must crosscheck with the word of God or Holy Bible. In doing so, we don't fall prey. Remember: the antics of the thief, the killer, the liar, the accuser and the destroyer. In short: don't get deceived again and again. Beware of things that are too good to be true.

Acceptance of Temptation

Gen. 3:6 *And when the woman saw that the tree was good for food, and that it was pleasant to the eyes, and a tree to be desired to make one wise, she took of the fruit thereof, and did eat, and gave also unto her husband with her, and he did eat.* Verses 2-4; is the **temptation** (deception and lies), Satan's sales talk, **the first part of SIN.** This can be construed as Satan's continued disobedience or opposition to God (his Creator), lust for power, and vengeance on His maker that resulted in casting him out into darkness as punishment. Obviously Satan and his demons are suffering the consequences of their disobedience. I would believe they are always in constant pain and torture.

Sad part is that, Eve was totally clueless and offered very little opposition to the temptation,

Verse 5: Satan sales talk is almost complete, man's weakest points was attacked and Eve has no where to go but yield.

Verse 6: **The second part of Sin is acceptance of temptation:** Eve accepts the temptation when she took and ate of the forbidden fruit. The fruit was laden, with spiritual poison seed put in place by Satan. The SIN of Eve is now complete. Eve was deceived, big time.

At this point of the temptation process, Adam could have simply told Satan to leave them alone, Satan would. Adam has more power than Satan in that instant because God was with him.

If Adam rejected the temptation by not partaking of the fruit, would Eve's Sin affect Adam? I believe not? Adam and Eve were married in the Garden of Eden by God and they lived as one body, and Adam as the head of the marriage. They are family.

See **I Cor. 11:3.** Apostle Paul says: *And I would have you know, that the Head of every man is Christ (authority); and the Head of the woman is the man (creation model sequence) and the Head of Christ is God the Father.* a separation of function of two of Godhead person. Finally, Adam partakes of the forbidden fruit given by Eve.

The acceptance by Adam completes the SIN of man.

I Tim 2:14, *And Adam was not deceived.* Adam's acceptance of the temptation, basically constitute a rebellion and disobedience to God's commandment. For Adam has the seed of God in his heart and mind. He has enough knowledge. I would believe, God would not leave him alone. And surely, he knows the consequences in disobeying God. The Words of God is True. He surely died.

The weakest points of Man: cravings for lust, power, and food and still true unto this day.

Definition of Sin

Sin has two parts: 1) It is a Temptation by Satan. 2) Man's acceptance of Satan's Lie. Man cannot sin by himself. The union of Satan and man will consummate sin and will separate man from his Creator God, and it is the reason, why we are experiencing **all** these problems. Man's desires alone, does not constitute a Sin if not by virtue of Satan's temptation. Most vices are not a sin because it only pleases man's own body, it is not meant to hurt anyone. I know, most very religious people will disagree with me. I believe God is not legalistic. God prefers worship rather than sacrifice.

The reason why the Bible says that God cannot look at sin: When man is in sin, he walks with Satan. Of course God is jealous that He lost His most precious creation to His adversary. Love hurts. God will look the other way. But it does not mean He does not love us anymore. It is also the very reason He sent His only begotten son Jesus to redeem us. God's feeling is the same as when we lose a loved one. It hurts. So, if we have a right frame of mind, why would we hurt our Father's feelings? We should love our Father, because He loved us first. Then we are assured that we are in good hands.

Consequences of SIN

The Adamic Covenant and Curses brings forth severe punishment to all involved. At this point Adam has committed the sin of fornication and spiritual adultery for having Satan as his companion where he affirmed his allegiance. Rather he must be eternally married to his Creator, our Jesus Christ.

Gen. 3:14 *To the serpent, upon your belly shall you go, and dust shall you eat all the days of your life.*

Gen. 3:15 *And I will put enmity between you and the woman; and between your seed and her seed shall bruise your head and you shall bruise His Heel.* This Prophecy was fulfilled; by Christ the seed of Mary at Calvary. The Cross of Christ crushed the head of Goliath (the seed of Satan) giving Him Victory over Satan, but Jesus feet were also bruised, "nailed to the Cross." King David buried the head of Goliath at Calvary hence the place is called Golgotha.

Gen. 3:16, *Unto the woman, He said, I will greatly multiply your sorrow and your conception; in sorrow shall you bring forth children;* ***and your desire shall be unto your husband and he shall rule over you.*** At this point the equality between a man and a woman: was removed by God. In today's society, women are clamoring for equality in this sinful world. They don't realize it is not going to happen. They can receive fairness but not equality. It will not happen in totality as they hope for. The curse is still on.

Equality, only exist in the context of God's love to His creation. After Adam's sin, equality was lost.

Gen. 3:17; *To Adam, God said, because you have hearkened unto the voice of your wife and have eaten of the tree; of which I commanded you, saying, you shall not eat of it; cursed is the ground for your sake;* "When God restored the earth, it was paradise with free flowing blessings to the inhabitants of it, but with man's Sin it will only provide reluctantly to their needs." *in sorrow shall you eat of it all the days of your life.* "It is now appointed unto man once to die". Proclaims the death sentence, all as a result of spiritual death.

Gen. 3:18 *Thorns also and thistle shall it bring forth to you, and you shall eat of the herb of the field.* The thorns signifies: Hard labor, Pain, tribulations, sickness, trials, sorrow and all sorts of problem, man has to suffer and endure.

Gen. 3:19 *In the sweat of your face shall you eat bread, till you return unto the ground* (mortal death); *for out of it you were taken: for dust you are, and unto dust shall you return.*

Now Satan possesses the spirit of Adam and Eve, and they are in bondage (walking side by side) to him (SIN); **It is virtual separation from God.** Man is now indebted to Satan.

And Adam and Eve were expelled from the Garden of Eden. (The Garden of Eden is in Paradise a Holy place, and Paradise can also mean as Jesus Christ).

Rom. 2:8 *But unto them who are contentious, **and do not obey the Truth**, but obey unrighteousness, indignation and wrath.* We oppose God's ways.

Rom. 2:9 *Tribulation and anguish, upon every soul of man who does evil, of the Jew first, and also of the Gentiles.* When we die as sinners and did not secure our salvation while we are still alive in our flesh, this is what our spirit and soul will experience: Tribulation and anguish. Suffering to the nth degree, ouch! Read Matt. 22:13; 24:51.

Prov. 8:36 *But he who sin against me wrongs his own soul: all they who hate me love death.* By sinning against or opposing God, you are hurting, or destroying your own soul. And if you hate God you love death; that you love that your soul will suffer in hell. If you love suffering in hell, then you are one crazy person.

Satan Rules

The seed of Satan now rules in man. Adam lost his dominion on earth and was now in the hands of Satan. Adam gave away his inheritance. By virtue of this exchange, Satan's number is now 6, and Adam's number is 5. Adam is now a captive of Satan and Sin (in bondage).

Now Man has to work the ground for food, in all his life. If I was Adam I would have divorced Satan long time ago, problem is we cannot on our own.

Rom. 6:23 *For the wages of Sin, is death; but the gift of God is eternal life through Jesus Christ Our Lord.* For the unbeliever, he would not feel or believe that this statement is ever true. Our first instinct would be, how can this happen? We will say, bull! I am totally alive, and I can do anything with my body, I can dance, sing, read or whatever. This Holy book they are talking about is just pulling my leg. I don't buy it.

But wait. Let us examine ourselves.

1) At some point in the life of man, one thing is sure to happen. We all die in this flesh and bones we so revere. Even how much money we spent to maintain and to sustain our way of life, as we know it. Still aging takes place and nothing we do can stop it. Then we are perplexed at why is death happening to all. We think there is no comprehensive explanation whatsoever.

2) Then as we age in the 40+, after we have accumulated some wealth from working too hard and hassle for advantage day in and day out, we start to feel some void in our lives. A feeling of longing and emptiness occupies our emotions and minds. Then we occupy ourselves; with activities that fascinates us like yoga, and other forms of eastern meditation. Still we are missing something. Finally we come to our senses; if we had not hardened our hearts yet. The True God is now calling us home. Thank someone, for somebody has prayed for you to come to God. Then we start seeking the Kingdom of God and now we understand that **Romans 6:23** is true.

Satan can have it his Way, if we allow it:

Luke 22:31 *And the Lord said, Simon, Simon, behold, Satan hath desired to have you, that he may sift you as wheat:* I don't believe that Satan asked permission from God to tempt Peter. Satan tempts to destroy, but God test us to bring out the best in us. By all means we must reject temptation even how much it looks good. Our rejection of the deception will weaken the evil spirits around us daily.

Luke 22:32 *But I have prayed for thee, and that thy faith fail not: and when thou art converted, strengthen thy brethren.* Now that we are waiting for the Second Advent of Christ, and with all the wisdom Christ has given unto us, we should be able to say NO to Satan's temptations, lies and deceptions on a consistent basis. And by our resolve: that we serve as an example to other brothers and sisters, especially to those who are starting to seek the **Kingdom of God.**

Where is the Lake of Fire: I believe it is like the Sun. Or it is really the sun? Always burning. Would you like your spirit to spend eternal life in such condition? I pray not.

CHAPTER 7

The Redeemer

In Adam: **Rom. 5:12** *Wherefore, as by one man's sin entered into the world, and death by sin* (both spiritual and physical death; because man is a three part being*) and so death was passed upon all men, for that all have sinned*:

Rom. 5:13 *(For until the Law sin was in the world: but sin is not imputed when there was no Law.*

Rom. 5:14 *Nevertheless death reigned from Adam to Moses, even over them who had not sinned after the similitude of Adam transgression, who is the figure of Him Who was to come.* One man's Sin makes all his next generation **sinners** until a redeemer comes (fulfilled about 2000 years ago). Man cannot redeem himself because he does not have the power to defeat Satan by himself, and until now we are still indebted to him. The very reason we need a Redeemer. Only God can defeat Satan.

Therefore, the redeemer must also be God. In the second Adam, Jesus Christ: The universal process of redemption; is completing the spiritual legalistic condition, by sacrifice involving the shedding of Sinless Blood at Calvary. **Blood Covenant is now fulfilled at the Cross of Christ.**

And by Faith and Faith alone in Christ, that man can be welcomed back to the presence of his Creator.

The spiritual exchange of possession can now take place for the better.

Without God on our side, we cannot defeat Satan; he is more powerful than us. This is especially true in the Old Testament time when there was no intercessor for the Jews yet on a regular basis. They, the Jews are always a loser in all battles that they fought on their own, revealed in stories after stories of defeat. But with God's assistance and intervention they win all the time. A manifestation: that there is a God, whose love is enough to protect those who Comes unto Him.

At present, in this Church Age or dispensation of grace period, we are extremely blessed to have Jesus Christ to fight our battles on a daily basis. Available 24/7/366.

The Scriptures says that God cannot look at SIN. Some Bible scholars, says it is because God is three times Holy, but I believe that a man in SIN is in bondage with Satan. Why would God look at Satan His enemy? If we are in sin, Father God cannot look at us. Although He can hear our cry for help, but He cannot do much until we repent of our sins, accept Jesus' offer of grace as a free gift and call on His Name.

Notes: I apologize for repeating words and certain phrases. My reason is that it has to be. Jesus repeats words like Verily, Verily, to put emphasis on very important things. And it is also the same, in this book. The purpose of Chapter 1-6 is to make known to All would be readers of this book, (the font are bigger to put emphasis and for the elderly be able to read without eye aid) the imperative importance of placing man's faith in the one true God, and in the right direction, so as none of us will be deceived by Satan and his cohorts **again**, who deceives anyone that they can. So I have to drill hard on the real eternal spiritual life issues, over and over in this book into the minds and hearts of all who might read, to separate eternal spiritual truth from the spiritual lies of our Maker's enemy.

Our spiritual life is so **precious** that we must spend a lifetime making it right with God and us being watchful all the time. Daily prayer asking our Father for supplication and protection will help us a lot. Jesus calls this putting on the Armor of God. The **Body of Christ** is our Armor and Shield.

See **John 14:6** *Jesus said, I am the Way, the Truth, and the Life: no one comes to the Father, but by Me.*

> **He declares that He is the only Way to the Father God. Positively no other.**

Jesus' Purpose in His First Advent

Jesus came so that All; might be saved, and fulfill His Promise, kept His Covenant with Abraham, so that God can claim back His most precious creation in man from the evil one at the time of Divine Appointment. See John 3:16.

In today's world, where problems abound, the only solution is Jesus Christ. Why do we keep on rejecting God's free gift of Grace? And when we are in trouble, we forget to come to Him and take refuge. Why do we insist on doing it our way, (only Burger King can say that, come on, smile a little bit) when we can really boast of nothing? Don't tell me you are filthy rich! God still owns all of what you have or posses. What are we trying to prove?

To whom: Cast out Satan away from your hearts, from your life, from your homes, and re-new your mind and body. In this way you remove the evil spirits that is blocking the blessings you must receive from the Father. Get your rest in Jesus' name (Sabbath). (I get my rest in a secret place). He is faithful!

The God of Abraham, Isaac and Jacob is a good God. He does not use force or intimidation in calling us to His Kingdom. He uses orderly process in giving us His words of wisdom in the Holy Bible. The Finished Work of Christ at the Cross: is the means to redeem his lost children.

Compare that to other forms of religion, especially the allah of Islam, where it uses force and intimidation to convert people of other faith. Look at the history of Islam. I don't believe that it is a religion of peace and love. When I was in Saudi Arabia in 1980, I know they don't have an Arabic word for love. What is happening in Iraq and Syria is hard to understand, for those who do not study their history. Connect the dots. June, 2014

Therefore, I pray to my God, that my potential brothers who are still in these other faiths be called into the Kingdom of Jesus Christ. Unless they come to Christ, I cannot call them brothers or sisters, because we will not be dwelling in the same place. The saints and I are in a place called Paradise where the ways of life is Holy. Amen.

Whereas, if my potential brothers keep their old belief or religion then they will be going to Hell, where there is weeping, wailing and gnashing of teeth, which means they are suffering.

Read **Matt. 13:42** The Son of Man: *And shall cast them into a furnace of fire: there shall be wailing and gnashing of teeth.* The furnace of fire is Hell (pre millenium period) is not the same as Lake of Fire (after the millennial kingdom). Also check out Matt.8:12 and Luke 13:28.

CHAPTER 8

The Great Debate

The Truth and The False

If truth is, there is no God, and man developed through evolution, man and other forms of life in this earth, came into being by chance and acquired life on it own according to Charles Darwin and company and not a creation by a God, then man has no spirit just like any other life form, if this is so, then there is no problem in dying spiritually or mortally. No possible eternal spirit life to worry about. Man's life is nothing and has no value, we should not struggle to look good or be good looking in the eyes of our fellow man, if this is the case, there is no right or wrong, then all has the right to kill one another with no accountability and chaos can abound? Would you, atheist man prefer a life like this, a life on earth with no order?

How would an atheist man react to this scenario? Shall he just rely on himself, on others or in government for protection? Why would anyone need protection, life is useless anyway according to atheist thinking! Damn if you do, or damn if you don't believe!

It will be pure hypocrisy for an atheist not to admit, all of us desperately need peace and order. Everyone is a beneficiary of the Bible's prescribe way of living in peace. God is hurting when He sees us, the apple of His eye, suffering. This is the very reason why Jesus Christ has to come to earth to save us from further suffering and humiliations. God has to restore and reconcile man to Him. Amen

Life will have no meaning. Why struggle to have a healthy life (exercise daily, and grab all the herbal medicine, and wellness products at GNC)? What are we working for so hard to have a better life? Why seek the American dream? There is no hope at all anyway? I can go on and on and on to tell all these negatives. I know no one wants to hear. But as man, do we want to cling and dwell on all these nothings? To the atheists: what is your sense of purpose? Do you think you are wiser than a believer in the True God, or just another fool?

This is what I know. I love my fellow man because every one is a potential brother or sister, if and only if all can be in the **Body of Christ.** You cannot be my brother if you are with Satan because you are going to a different world, the Lake of Fire.

According to King Salomon: What we reap from the desires of our flesh is: Vanity, vanity, and vanity.

Another problem: Man perceives that science is everything we need to know, because we are not taught in school that science is from God. The almighty God is science. But the irony is, in the daily lives of the unbeliever, they enjoy all the benefits of orderly living brought about by the value of Judeo Christian faith.

Which is the very foundation of life with God in this earth. What they don't want to do is accept God. This attitude is definitely influenced by Satan whose evil seed is in man at this moment in time. This evil seed in man will be here on earth; until Jesus comes the second time and defeat Satan once and for all in the Battle of Armageddon. Jesus and His saints bind him up and throw Satan into the bottomless pit, where he will suffer for a millennium for his sin against God.

What facts? Satan wants us to know and accept is, that there is no God. Satan is the thief, the killer, the destroyer, and the deceiver. The worst part is that he is the king of this earth for all bad measure.

For Adam gave away man's dominion of earth in his fall from grace at the Garden of Eden.

The First Amendment, US Constitution

Congress shall make no law respecting an establishment of religion, ...

The First Amendment is not articulated right. **It must be interpreted this way: Separation of State and Church. There is no such thing as Separation of Church and State,** a big lie by the enemy, emissaries of evil, the ACLU. This group created a stumbling block for the Church.

Remember this always: The US Constitution was promulgated by our founding Fathers, that the citizens of the Federation must be protected at all cost. It mostly spells what the State can and cannot do. Especially at the Executive Branch and the Judiciary, it should refrain from making executive orders and edicts. We have a Congress to make the Laws of the Land.

The restriction is on the State, not on the Church. The Church is not restricted from getting involved with the State or government affairs. The Church can use government facilities for whatever they desire, because it is the Church (people) who paid for all these government facilities. Even atheist, are welcomed to use it for whatever purpose they desire.

Why? Because, the State cannot exist: If there is no Church (The people who believes in the one True God). Whereas; the Church can exist without the State. The State cannot exclude People with Right Faith. It is these people with the Right Faith who created the State. The people created the State (government). Is the creation greater than the creator? It must not happen. If it does, then chaos everywhere will abound. That is happening to USA right now. There is very low morality of government officials. The love of power is prevailing rather than love and service to the country.

It is these Church (people) that created the State and thus allowed order to prevail and gave meaning to Life; that Life is Sacred.

In essence; the First Amendment's purpose is to protect the Church. The Constitution did not give the Church a right to have a military force. That power was given to the State, to protect and serve the Church (people); who are paying so called taxes, (the people are simply pooling their money, so that big projects, like the military, roads and bridges can be done) so that they are protected. But now what is the State doing? Now it is against and ruling the Church, the Church (People) must rule. I wonder where are our so-called brilliant Constitutional Attorneys to protect the Citizens of USA. Our present voters are becoming dumber and dumber for allowing this to happen. What happened to our government of the people, for the people and by the people? My feeling is that: we Americans are losing it now and only the powerful few in the government rules. We are just like any 3rd world country.

Honestly my take on these is: that Satan is getting a stronghold on our government now. **Wake Up America;** we must bring back our Lord Jesus Christ in the midst our government. Our public official or our public servants must have moral integrity and spiritual accountability.

The State is called Public Servants: If I visit the President at the White House; basically I can ask him to shine my shoes. Right? And he should do it without blinking. I am the Public; He is the servant. Right? Just to make a point.

The ACLU and other leftist organizations have twisted and tampered the Truth. Worst result is; Americans and the rest of the world bought into it. **Blindly.** Why are we allowing the ACLU and other communist organization to have it their way? They are the minority. This country was founded on the platform of majority rules.

Thomas Jefferson is partly to blame for bad articulation of the First Amendment in his correspondence to call for **"a wall of separation between Church and State."** They used the bad articulation; to stumped on the inalienable rights of the people

(Church). Where are the ACLJ, constitutional experts and lawyers to articulate this rights for the American people? Where is the Supreme Court?

With this State's hostile attitude against the Church, the Church (people) have the right to deny giving taxes to the State. Why? Elected government officials and employees of the State especially in the Judiciary Department have virtually turned against the main source of their existence, the Church. Talking about biting the hands that feeds. This is the work of evil who, does not know how to repay with gratitude.

And if you teach Theory of Evolution in Public Schools, it must be accompanied with a disclaimer. And to be fair, Creation model of the Holy Bible must also be taught alongside with this theory. That will give our children informed decision on what to believe. Since the government gives equal opportunity in almost any aspect, then this area must be given the same privilege and attention. Do not force this theory into our throats. Satan is always unfair. You, the State is very unfair. The present executive branch is the most corrupt as it has deceived the people most.

Reminder: The US Constitution is an inspired Word of God. It does not promise equality, but rather fairness. A level playing field is needed so that everybody has a chance to be the best to excel and be productive and realize whatever dreams (The American Dream) they may have.

A Republic was born. Exactly how the God of the Judeo-Christian Faith wants it done. Let the flame of our American Dream live forever.

We must not allow the communist and socialist to destroy America, because they carry the vile of God's enemy. These people are **promoting equality,** not in this sinful world. There is no such thing as equality in this world, for none of us was born equal. It is an evil façade. Let us not fall for it. We can only experience equality in the **Kingdom of Jesus Christ.** In Heaven there is a King (King of the Jews. We will all become Jews. There is no difference between Jews and Gentiles). As **Members of the Kingdom of God;** we have different functions and purposes. God's Love is same for all of us. It is the only thing I know we have equality.

In this world, we are different from one another, and we have different capacity to achieve whatever work we do. How can we achieve equality in this world? Don't even try. Satan wants us to believe it can happen. Equal opportunity? Maybe Yes.

Theory of Evolution:

Inasmuch that I hate to talk and discuss this issue, I believe I owe it to our young people who are in High School and in Universities and Colleges that they are being deceived big time by the Department of Education. The teachers and their professors are teaching our children junk information. That life on Earth is just about flesh, blood and bones. That science is just science and God, the Divine Creator has nothing to do with it.

Truth is: Science is God's. Without God there is no Science. Who are this scientist' trying to fool?

What most educators don't want to accept is: there is a Spiritual side of Life. They don't believe that God's creation model belong in our Public Schools and it has to be discarded. This thinking is mainly fueled by ACLU's assertion that there is a separation between Church and State. Man's life in this earth has two sides. Spiritual and there is also a mortal aspect. A coin has always two sides as well.

To the proponents (claiming to be experts) of this theory, just once: **I challenge you, show us your expertise, not just all talk.** (I know you experts will despise me). Prove to me that monkeys and apes can procreate with humans: Or a goose and an eagle: Or a cat and a dog? **The apes could not take on a new shape or form by itself.** It will remain an ape forever. The same thing will happen to the goose and the cat. Show me result of experiments not by observation alone. Although every one is entitled to his own. Even cars, airplanes, or any man made tools will not evolve, man created them. Man creates new shapes or size of a car or airplane and should not be considered as form of evolution? The old car cannot take on a new shape by itself. Man has to make the changes. Just like God, He is the only one who can transform Man, His creation from sinner to holy.

Man has already created billions of things that we are using every day. God also created billions of stars, plants, animals and sand, that we can see everyday. Therefore, God and Man are both creators. There is no way it could happen with the Theory of Evolution based on random chance of making it? What an irony. Truth is Darwin and company can make a mistake. God cannot lie.

Totally, this is the work of Satan that is meant to deceive man. It is a trap set up by Satan to keep man away from God and to bring animosity between man and his Maker. This theory; are for the fools. The wise recognizes the fact that there is a Divine God and will not believe this theory.

Up to the present time, the theory of evolution remains a theory. No scientist or any man who firmly believes has come up with the proof that this so called scientific theory is true. And yet; it is being taught in schools as facts. It should not be. They say there is a missing link. What missing link? Plainly, **there is no life link.** If there is a link, how come until now, no scientist can come up with evidence, and show it for the whole world to see. Anywhere?

The **Theory of Evolution is Satan's number one (1) deception tool.** His objective is to poison the minds and hearts of young people. And the idea has been embraced by the educated people and academia, with pride and lust for power, and proclaimed that it is fact and it is complete science. They declared the theory was already proven by nature even without doing any empirical experiment. Mere observation of the habitat of animals and their survival of the fittest is not enough to prove the idea. It is a very flawed thinking relying solely on an idea based on assumption. Then concluding that it is the key that proves evolution is already a fact. Example: How can a small animal overrun or fight a bigger animal, even how much more fit is the smaller one. Over 90% of the time; the smaller animal don't stand a chance to survive. Therefore the idea of survival of the fittest does not hold water. It is a flawed assumption.

Theory Evolution is of Evil; which is also false. To the US Department of Education: STOP: Teaching this none sense. STOP: Deceiving our children by teaching this unproven theory in our public schools as facts. Or teach God's Creation model alongside as well. Another problem is that parents do not teach their children at home about the wisdom in believing in the One True God, the God of Abraham, Isaac and Jacob. This is the most **profitable wisdom** for all.

CHAPTER 9

Who is Satan?

What Are His Characters?

We have to explore this topic so we know what to avoid and be not deceived again, and again, and again.

Satan: Besides being the serpent.

Eph. 2:2 *Wherein in time past you walked according to the course of this world, according to the **prince of the power of the air,** the spirit that now works in the children of disobedience.* (**This verse says that Satan is the head of world's system**)

Eph. 2:3 *Among whom we all had our conversation in times past in the lust of our flesh and of the mind; and were by nature the children of wrath, even as others.* If we are not watchful of our **Spiritual Wellbeing** at all times, he (Satan) can snatch us from the protection of our Lord Jesus, death can come to us without warning. Dying in an accident, heart attack; are examples of dying without warning. We do not want that happening.

Prince of the Power of the Air (as the destroyer)

Natural calamities that we experience like: the hurricanes of the Western Hemisphere, or typhoons of the Eastern Hemisphere, the Philippine Islands, and tornadoes (American mid-west) are all originated by the destroyer. Why are these calamities mostly prevalent in the USA and the Philippines? Any idea? These two countries are dwelling places for God. The enemy wants to destroy them but he will not succeed.

These calamities have destroyed and inflicted more pain and destruction than any other disasters the world has ever known. The frequency that it is happening now is way higher than in any other time.

Prince of the Power of the Air
(as the Killer of Life on Earth):

In the air we breathe everyday, there is a killer that comes along with it. The air is supposed to keep us alive and well, but no. True, without oxygen in the air we cannot survive in this planet. But this air kills man really slow, but surely man will die.

The air element is called Oxidant, a positively charge oxygen ion. It is the element that oxidizes steel, and in the process of oxidation, the steel will rust and eventually be destroyed. The same process happens to living things like animals, and plants they all die.

Many people have asked this question. Doctor, why do people get sick? I assume doctors know the answer instead they run around the bush and will not answer directly. They want to keep it a secret knowledge.

Their closest answer is the environment. Some will answer with toxins, bacteria, virus, lifestyle and etc. These are the most common. I believe the best answer is Oxidant; more than 90% of the reason, why people get sick and die. Just imagine, that in every breath we take, there are oxidants in the air. No wonder the Holy Bible says: It is appointed unto man once to die. There is no escape. Proof that God knows everything.

To slow down this process: the cure: is Anti-oxidant. Yes, we have heard about this hyphenated word so much. My question is: do we understand what it is? Anti-oxidants are elements; that are negatively charged. The best anti-oxidant elements are mineral ions. Please check your high school science book, why? Ok, don't bother. I will explain. Just fasten your seat belts.

Take the positively charge oxygen ion (air), and negatively charge mineral ions. Question: what will happen if these two meet. I consider these two elements as two kids with ADHD; very hyperactive. Since an atom is actually a magnet, the two ions will be attracted to each other forming a mineral oxide. They have a very strong affinity for each other. I call it cell polarization or cell balancing. Now the new compound is now inert or neutral. Once the Oxidant is rendered neutral, it cannot hurt our body. But how many Oxidants do we take in daily?

Nobody knows at this time. My estimate is we take on more oxidants than we take in anti oxidants on a 2:1 ratio. Obviously, we cannot escape death we can only slow it down. This explains why the Holy Spirit says: It is now appointed unto man once to die. Oxidants are the # 1 killer of man.

But we will say: Why would God allow man to suffer and die if He is really a good God and loves His creation man? What we fail to consider is that God gave man Free Will.

Here is the answer: As Apostle Paul puts it in a perfect perspective: We have to die or be divorced from our old self in order for our creator to sanctify us. You see, Satan has impregnated our minds and flesh with his evil seed and rendered it corrupt. Don't you see yourselves in the mirror? Most of the time we act like Satan too. We hate our fellow man. We are mean to each other and we envy and enjoy when we hurt or kill one another, and so on. Thank God. He does not want any of this crap in our body.

That is why Christ has to make us into a new creation if we accept His amazing grace. We cannot enter into His Kingdom if He cannot sanctify us. Dying in the flesh and bones has to happen. So God can give us everlasting life. If you do not want eternal life, there is nothing I can help you with. Neither Jesus can help you."

Here's why people get sick: When the Oxidant gets into our body, it will look for un-polarized cells, meaning unbalanced cells and it will steal the negative ion of that cell. And once the cell lost a negative ion, that cell will be rendered weaker or unbalanced by the loss. Unbalanced cells will not regenerate balanced or healthy cells. Over time more and more cells in our body does not have the ability to regenerate, we call it aging. Or worse we get sick, suffer diseases that are hard to cure. Eventually we die.

Most diseases like cancer, diabetes, and you name it are all hastened or triggered by Oxidants. Sad part is we think of it as being caused by something else. Actually we can blame Satan. Not God. Therefore, our health objective must be, how to secure **Spiritual Wellness** rather than Physical Wellness. On instinct we usually choose the latter.

Where do Mineral Anti-Oxidants come from? They come from the ground. We can get it especially from root crops like potatoes, fruits, seeds, grains, herbs and vegetables. Some naturally occurring non- metallic minerals are very good source of Anti-oxidants. But be very careful, as they are not created equal. It has to be tested with total caution. The ground is our source of life. It is our Father God. He rested on the 7th day, so with us.

We have our own Mineral Anti-oxidants: eM+ Power Herbs. www.Z88-88ph.com

What about from meat? Yes we need meat for our source of protein to build muscles and some minerals like iron and calcium, but virtually no anti oxidant present.

The above paragraph; shows us that Anti-Oxidant is a temporary solution, but it also comes from our Father God as our Jehovah Jireh. The real solution is Christ.

Ezek. 15:2 *Son of Man,* *What is the vine tree more than any tree, or than a branch which is the trees of the forest?* The vine tree in this verse, refers to false gods (Satan); he also pretends to be a true tree to deceive many, and actually are only good to make fire. It will not bear good fruit. Its branches are wild and are the Sinners; this is the Tree of Knowledge of Good and Evil.

John 10:10 *The thief comes not, but to steal; and to kill, and to destroy.* This is the work of Satan, to deceive and to accuse man of his bad past and his emissaries (demons) are peddling them to mankind. So we must be wary of their deeds and we must reject them at all cost, otherwise we will remain dead in our spirit. And we will lose our chance to be with our Father again who loves us.

Corruption is Evil Inspired:

Most people don't take this sin very seriously, especially in the third world countries. Taken for granted so much, that it destroy the very core of the existence of their government and their citizens.

If the government is corrupt, the blessing of God to that country is also being withheld, and the earth is reluctant in giving up its wealth. The whole country becomes poor.

Corruption by Government Officials

And by head of state is one of the most devastating of all Corruption. God can withhold the blessings that a nation or country can receive from God. God will bless whosoever He wants. He will bless those that obey His statutes. Most people don't realize that corruption kills the business environment, kills the moral of constituency, and kills all things related to prosperity. Thereby most of their citizens live in poverty. Therefore we must elect only men and women with high moral integrity. Example:

Mexico, Somalia, Philippines, Indonesia, Sudan, Venezuela and many African countries.

Corruption by Private Businesses

As well, are becoming extremely corrupt and greedy for material wealth by paying ultra low wages and offer no fringe benefits either to their employees. I don't think they realize that they have been riding on the backs of working people, taking advantage of the free ride already too long. They don't realize the suffering of the working class, and they don't see the sweat and blood flowing on their eyebrows. The guilty of these sins, are mostly Chinese Corporations of Communist China. They employ espionage, bribery to government officials of other countries, especially in countries stricken with poverty. Time will come, they will have to pay back seven times to the people they have oppressed. Read Exodus.

Other forms of corruptions:

1) Corruption of the minds of minors.

Pedophiles are most guilty and they are so many.

2) Teaching the Theory of Evolution:

Is a form of Corruption: A false theory, which is not yet scientifically validated. For it to be taught in the under 18 years old and below students of Public Schools, is not acceptable. It is one of the worst forms of corruption. Something that is not a fact must be removed. There must be a disclaimer.

It affects millions of young Americans and millions more abroad and will take decades to undo the damage. The Christian community must take the lead role in undoing the damage.

The managers of the US Department of Education are not seeing the bad telltales; that is happening in their watch. There are too many incidents of killings of young children in schools. I just don't know what will it take to wake up these administrators of impending chaos to happen in the future. What these administrators and educators don't know or don't want to acknowledge is that these events are spiritually orchestrated by evil.

3) **Communism: The evil inspired dogma:**

In the former USSR, during the cold war, I remember, the Russian people have no freedom. No freedom of speech, no freedom of religion, no freedom to travel abroad, and all the people is to work only for the Communist State. But the Communist Party leaders are having the time of their lives, living in plenty, whereas the working people are living on provisions of barely enough. And they say there is equality. The party leaders have been riding on the backs of the poor citizen. They must revolt.

In the 1980's, they ran out of flour and bread was rationed. And America provided the much needed flour, even though USA and USSR are having a cold war. America had shown the world of her true colors as a country with compassionate leadership and made me proud that I am an American.

Look at North Korea, Cuba, Venezuela, Russia and China: the leaders of these countries are still clinging to Communism ideology that does not work. The ideology that is only good for people who are in power. For the common people there is nothing. There is no proof of prosperity in return for submitting to the powerful few.

In America, God instituted a Republic so that every citizen has a voice and is involved in managing the Republic as they choose. In God We Trust.

What I don't understand is why the people of these countries still don't get it. Communism does not do any good for those who aspire of a better life. That is why, the people of Communist countries who has big dreams comes to USA. Communism is good for lazy people.

4) Socialism: Another Evil Inspired System.

Socialistic form of government, are boasting that they champion redistribution of wealth to the poor. Sure the poor needs a lifeline to get off poverty. But the lifeline must only be temporary. Good work should be encouraged and are not.

Socialism teaches reliance on government for measly handouts rather than on God's unlimited blessings. Taking funds from the hard workers, innovators, inventors and business people and then give to takers and lazy. This type of governance gets its way by imposing high taxes. But once the source of funds run dry, economic chaos sets in. Example: Europe. Countries that required bailouts: Greece, Portugal, Spain and many more on the brink of insolvency. The purpose of the elected government officials is to enable them to perpetuate themselves in endless power over the people. Employing a political system driven by greed and evil.

Rev. 12:10…. *For the accuser of our brethren is cast down, which accused them before our God day and night.* (This is Satan's work 24/7/365.)

I tell my children at the dinner table: If your professor is teaching something new, do not believe their statement right away. Always benchmark their words against what the Bible says. If, it's validated true and correct then say OK. By doing it this way, you will not be deceived.

CHAPTER 10

Proof of Creation

It is so much easier to show billions and billions of evidence for the creation model rather than evolution theory. We can see billions of sand, stars in the sky, trees, animals and people of different races created by God. All things work in balance. How much more evidence do we want? How can man dispute the claims of his maker? **What about: just show me evidence for Theory of Evolution that existence by random chance, can actually happen?** Just 1. There is none, until now.

Furthermore, the Holy Bible has proven itself with numerous accounts of prophecies that have come to pass. Countless miracles performed by Jesus and until this day and age, miracles are happening in front of our very eyes. These miracles were documented; by various historians and disciples of Jesus Christ. Anyone who has ears, let them hear and anyone who has the eyes let them see, and believe, and can document the daily miracles that are happening in this Church Age.

I could not believe. So many college graduates, so many highly educated people, are being deceived big time. And taken for a very long ride by Satan. Not knowing, who God is? Almost three fourths of the world's population does not know and understand the economy of their Creator. The next verse best describes those claiming to be wise.

Wise Men:

Rom. 1:21-23 *Because that, when they knew God, they glorified Him not as God, neither were thankful; but became vain in their imaginations, and their foolish hearts darkened. Professing themselves to be wise, they became fools. And changed the glory of the uncorruptible God into an image like to corruptible man, and to birds, and four footed beast, and creeping things.* Those people who proclaims that they are learned because of knowledge acquired from higher learning universities and don't acknowledge the Word of God are simply fools.

What if the truth is, there is a God:

That we are accountable to believe in Faith, in order to live an eternal life with our Creator. If we do not accept this fact even if it is spiritual; **then we are doomed forever, because we will be spiritually dead, separated from our Creator, eternal suffering in the Lake of Fire as the Bible has described. It will never hurt us to believe in God. We cannot lose. Why gamble?**

Psalm 9:17 *The wicked shall be turned into Hell, and all nations that forget God.* **The word "wicked" means; unbelievers, who oppose God, and who have heard about the Word of God and hardened their hearts, denies in his mind and heart, that God does exist.** Denial the Holy Spirit as God is an unforgivable sin.

It is the only unforgivable sin described in the Bible. So man must take heed, and believe the Word of God, the Truth (Jesus Christ) manifested and validated by the Holy Spirit.

John 3:16 *For God so loved the world, the He gave his only begotten Son, that whosoever believes in Him should not perish, but have everlasting life.*

There are many things that man does, that **is very spiritually holy,** that most of us don't even know or even cognizant of. For example:

1) If you respect and love your neighbors as your brothers and sisters.
2) If you forgive any one who trespasses against you. Or give the other cheek.
3) Be very considerate and compassionate to the needs of other people around you, or your neighbors.

Just to mention a few. Anything you do with Love.

The Choice

Now that we have established the facts, it's time to make a **Choice: Eternal Life, With God, Paradise or Eternal Death, Separation from God, Lake of Fire?** Where do you want to spend your Spirit Life? The Holy Bible was not written by the Holy Spirit through the Prophets to scare man, but rather to give man; informed decisions to make the right choice.

Spiritual Wellness vs. Health Wellness (Body)

Why would anyone want to play Russian roulette with his spirit and soul? It is like playing dare the Lake of Fire, absolutely not advisable to risk the **Health Wellness** of your spirit and fall from grace. Absolutely, there is nothing to lose to accept and believe.

Why risk? Acts 16:30 *And brought them out and said, Sirs, what must I do to be saved?*

Acts 16:31 *And they said, Believe on the Lord Jesus Christ, and you shall be saved.* Do we need more proof to believe? All we need is a little faith as big as a mustard seed. By God's love this little faith will grow.

My Personal Testimony:

About twenty-five years ago, I had a very vivid dream. I was walking in a gondola to board a work barge and I was met by Jesus on my left and by Satan on my right.

I was asked by both, who am I going to come with. I told Satan; I am not going with you. I choose Jesus Christ. Never would I forget that dream, 'cause I know that was the time when my Father in Heaven called me to be His adopted child.

It is a win-win situation for the Believers. I believe I have made it very clear to whosoever would read this book. Man's decision to accept and believe is actually a no brainer. Again:

Accepting and Believing in Jesus Christ is a Big No Brainer.

Let us not make the same mistake again and again and again; by copying what Adam and Eve did at the Garden of Eden. They disobeyed the Commandment of our Father God. Every time we allow Satan to deceive us, we eat the fruit of the Tree of Knowledge of Good and Evil again and we will surely die. Now we know full well the Consequences of Sin. It is devastating to our **Spiritual Wellbeing.** We must not disobey and oppose God again. This is my prayer.

Today we are very lucky for we have the means to commune with Our Creator through the Finished Work of Jesus Christ by dying and shedding His Blood at the Cross. We are saved. The best things that can happen to man are here. To be called as sons and daughters of God. To be called as Saints or Holy. To be called as Heirs of the Kingdom of God. My friends, my brothers and sisters, what more can we ask for? For Christ is sufficient.

The Choice is crystal Clear. Jesus.

Enough is said! It is my hope, that now, the reader will make the right Choice in Choosing to Follow God the Son, Jesus Christ, God's Love must be Our Choice:

If the reader does not choose God, you can stop reading now. I will be praying for you that you may finally accept God's calling.

The following Chapters are not for you to waste your time. You can dwell in the Lake of Fire. That is your choice and your own will. There is no other to blame, when you find out there is no more another chance for regret, cause you did receive this warning. Remember; regrets always comes when everything is said and done or at the end.

So better think again, real hard. While, you are still alive in the flesh. The Bible says, that the best things in this world are reserved for those who, believes in Jesus Christ NOW.

My last question for you: Do you want to go to Paradise or not? Our Father in Heaven is waiting for your YES answer. Please call on Him now, for tomorrow sometimes is too late. Jesus said don't delay your call on Him for another day. Now is the day.

I say: **Life is Short, Pray Hard**. Nike says otherwise.

CHAPTER 11

The Solution

Where Do We Begin: Seek Ye First the Kingdom of God, Matt. 6:33

Kingdom of God

In the Gospel of Matthew, the Bible gives us instructions how to: **Matt. 6:25-34;** The admonition of Jesus Christ says; **6:33** *But seek ye first the Kingdom of God, and his righteousness; and these things will be added unto you.* This verse, "Seek ye First" gives us the condition for, to receive God's blessings, His interests are to be "first". To acknowledge that He is our Lord and Savior and Him; Crucified; then He gives us the "guarantee of God's Provision" Also to acknowledge that the **Kingdom of God is Jesus Christ himself.** This answers the question Who, Where, What, is the Kingdom of God? If the seeker will start looking for the Kingdom of God and asks the question: Where or What? He will not find it. There is no way he can see it in the sky or see it physically on earth. But, the Who question will lead him to Jesus Christ and answers all three questions: What is the Kingdom of God? Where is the Kingdom of God? Who is the

Kingdom of God? The **Body of Christ is here on earth and it is growing every second.** Thanks for every believer who comes to Christ every second.

In this Church Age or Dispensation of Grace, there is no physical evidence of the Kingdom yet, but He will come. We have to visualize in the spiritual dimension to understand in order to worship God in spirit and in truth.

Check this out: "***his righteousness***" is not capitalized to denote that his work at the cross was done in total obedience to the will of the Father in Heaven, while Jesus was in the flesh. Only Jesus was able to perform and obey all the 613 commandments of God stated in the Old Testament, the 10 commandments included. To repeat: The Tallit or prayer shawl used by Jewish Rabbis, in every corner contains 613 knots to signify the number of commandments. The Tallit is also referred to as the "secret place".

If we acknowledge that Jesus is our Lord and Savior, we are also able to perform and obey all 613 commandments required by our Father in Heaven by Faith. Our acceptance and belief that Jesus is our Lord and Him Crucified and proclaims his death until He comes back again, guarantees our **"Justification by Faith".**

All our sins are forgiven; remembered no more and dump into the deepest part of the ocean and never to be brought up again. And now, we are declared by God; the Father as righteous, because, we are walking hand and hand with Jesus.

What a wonderful Promise by our Creator.

"and these things will be added unto you" If we read starting from **Matt. 6-26-32,** It states man's daily needs or "Daily Bread". God, the Father says we must not worry and He will supply every thing (enough food, clothing and shelter) if we do His commandments (pre-conditions). Putting our Faith only and only in Jesus Christ as our Lord.

How to Be Saved?

The conditions are:

How to Receive Christ: 1) Confess your Faith. Acknowledge that we are sinners.

Rom. 3:23 *For all have sinned, and come short of the glory of God.*

Rom. 10:9 *That if you shall confess with your mouth the Lord Jesus, and shall believe in your heart that God has raised Him from the dead, you shall be Saved.* Read also verses Rom. 10:10-11 to have a complete understanding of this part of the Scriptures.

Rom. 10:12 *For there is no difference between the Jew and the Greek: for the same Lord over all is rich unto all who call on Him.* No matter who you are.

2) Acknowledge and believe that Jesus Christ is Our Lord and Savior and Him Crucified.

1 Cor. 2:2 *For I determined not to know among you save Jesus Christ, and Him Crucified.*

3) Faithfully follow Christ ways until we die in the flesh. Finish the race.

Acts 20:24 *But none of theses things move me, neither I count my life dear unto myself, so that I might finish my course with joy, and the ministry, which I have receive of the Lord Jesus, to testify the Gospel of Grace of God.*

The following will happen to your whole being:

   a) A believer will have a born again experience. Transformation into a new creation, as in the water turned to wine in a wedding at Cana.
   b) Spiritual circumcision of the heart, a baptism by the Holy Spirit. Your heart will be cut open and blood will flow and Holy Spirit will come in with blood and a blood covenant will take place. This event will occur spiritually.
   c) You will become a **Member (cell) of the Body of Christ,** Read **Rom. 12.**
   d) You will be grafted in the One True Vine as a branch, **John 15:1-17**
   e) You will bear fruit. (There is also a pre-condition to receive uncommon blessings from the Father God. I will discuss later in the book).

Phil. 4:19 *But my God shall supply all your need, according to His Riches in Glory by Christ Jesus.* This is another incredible promise by Jesus. Imagine all His promise of prosperity not only in faith (love) but also in material things. He said it all.

In Acts 16:30 *And brought them out, and said, Sirs, what must I do to be saved.*

Acts 16:31 *And they said, Believe on the Lord Jesus Christ, and you shall be saved, and your house.*

This is the most direct and perfect explanation on how to obtain Salvation or Redemption from sin. It also explains that salvation is not limited to the individual believer but also available to the entire family (cell).

All members of the family are called by the Father to become believers in His Son as well. Now it is up to the individual to accept or reject the Divine Invitation. But Jesus will always seek the Lost Sheep.

Luke 17:20 says; *And when He was demanded of the Pharisees, when the Kingdom of God should come; He answered them and said. The Kingdom of God cometh not with observation,*

Luke 17:21 *Neither, shall they say, Lo here! Or, lo there! For, Behold, the Kingdom of God is within you.*

This verse validates the question: Who is the **Kingdom of God?** The Kingdom of God is Jesus Christ himself.

To the Jews, when Jesus came the first time, they claimed and are expecting that, when their Messiah comes, He will overthrow whoever is in power, conquering them, and at that time, it was the Romans. The Jews did not recognize Him as their Messiah. Jesus wept.

Believers (Churches)

Born-again Christians or believers in Christ, has the experience that brings Christ into their hearts and places the **Kingdom of God** within. Some calls this, the in dwelling of the Holy Spirit, which is also Jesus Christ, himself. The believers are also called appropriately as **Members of the Body of Christ.**

Christianity is not a Religion. It is a spiritual family relationship with God. In the Lord's Prayer, Jesus said we are to pray to Our Father. Therefore, being declared a **Member of the Body of Christ** confirms that relationship.

Eph. 3:17 *That Christ may dwell in your hearts by Faith; that you, being rooted and grounded in love.* The in dwelling of the Holy Spirit in our hearts starts a spiritual communion or relationship with God through Jesus Christ our Lord, "grounded in LOVE" satisfies the condition for Jesus to be in us and us in Him. This will start our relationship with our Creator God. Remember, everything we have, will always come only through Christ. There is NO If's or But's about it.

John 11:40 *Jesus said unto her, Said I not unto you that, if you believe, you should see the Glory of God?* In this Church Age, this is the appointed time, if we can only humble ourselves to submit and believe Jesus Christ as the Messiah; we can see the

"Glory of God". Nothing is impossible for man as there is nothing impossible for Our Father God.

The time to believe and accept Christ is NOW. We must not wait for tomorrow, for tomorrow may not come and we completely missed our chance.

No Equality

Our God is an Equal Opportunity God. God loves His creation equally, though they are not created the same. When God created man in His image, He created male and female. Where is the equality there? Women pushing for equality: is one of Satan's deceptive tools. God loves all equally, no matter what.

So never seek equality in this world, for no two men or person are equal. Any agenda pushing for equality between men and women will always fail: it is an evil ploy. It is better to accept and value each one, and on his own strength, to give integrity to each and to love one another. You will only be frustrated as there is no chance for equality to happen in this mortal world. We all have our own cross to carry. You have to love what God gives you, and with thanksgiving.

Fairness is available, but we have to work hard for it. As only very few men wants to extend an olive branch to any one, except those, that which I call 100 fold Christians, which are blessed by our Father in Heaven with unlimited gift of love in their hearts.

Unforgivable Sin:
Blasphemy Against the Holy Spirit

Matt. 12:22 *Then was brought unto Him one possessed with a devil (demon), blind and dumb; and He healed him, insomuch that the blind and the dumb spoke and saw. And the people were amazed, and said, Is not this the son of David?* Jesus healed the dumb and the blind, and the people were amazed, then someone said; Is not this the Son of David? Someone said this, because, he was led by the Holy Spirit. How would anyone know without the help of the Holy Spirit? King David lived about 1000 years before Christ came. And he knows.

Matt. 12:24 *But when the Pharisees heard it, they said, This fellow does not cast out devils, but by Beelzebub the prince of the devils.* Simply: a false accusation of Christ. They don't know who Christ is.

Matt. 12:25 *And Jesus knew their thoughts,* (a revelation from the Holy Spirit) *and said unto them, every kingdom divided against itself is brought to desolation; and every city or house divided against itself shall not stand.*

Thus, the saying, united we stand, united we fall and can't be vice-versa.

Matt 12:27 *And if by Beelzebub cast out devils, by whom do your children cast them therefore they shall be your judges.* The Pharisee accusation cannot stand, for its basis is false, therefore it backfired on them. Any other gods other than the God of Abraham, Isaac and Jacob are false, and here Jesus rebuked them teaching us the

Truth. Jesus equipped us with a solid knowledge about false gods and it is now up to us to choose the correct God to believe.

Matt. 12:28 *But if I cast out devils by the Spirit of God, then the Kingdom of God is come unto you.* By this statement the Pharisees should have been able to discern that the man they are talking to is the Messiah they have been waiting for. Pride kills.

Matt. 12:29 *Or else how can one enter the strong man's house, and spoils his goods, except he first bind the strong man and he will spoil his house.* Verse 29 is a prophecy that will happen after Armageddon, at the Day of Atonement when the **Body of Christ** shall bind Satan and send him to the bottomless pit for a thousand years so he cannot tempt and destroy man's holy relationship with Father God again.

Matt 12:30 *He who is not with Me is against Me; and he who gathers not with Me scatters abroad.* Anyone who is not a **Member of the Body of Christ** is not with Him, thus they are outside Christ influence and are just roaming around or scattered abroad or away from Christ. "he who gathers" means those who have a relationship with Christ, those who eats His broken bread of life and drink the wine, which signifies His shed blood, communes with Christ. At Pentecost the Holy Spirit descended unto Earth: The gathering of the Body of Christ has begun at Pentecost, which He gave up at the cross.

Therefore, it is very important to do the Lord's Supper, the eating of the broken bread as often as you can, to maintain our relationship with Christ. It allows us to focus our faith in Christ.

Matt. 12:31 *Wherefore, I say unto you, All manner of sin and blasphemy shall be forgiven unto men: but the blasphemy against the Holy Spirit shall not be forgiven unto men.* "Blasphemy against the Holy Spirit can only be committed by anyone who has understood and experience the Truth about God and then willfully opposed God. Example: Lucifer knows and understood the economy of God, he knows how the Holy Spirit works and then he opposed God. That is the reason why he cannot be forgiven ever, I believe even if he asked for forgiveness. Just like the Pharisees, they also understood and they opposed Jesus and blasphemed the Holy Spirit in the process, will not be forgiven. An uninformed man cannot commit blasphemy for lack of knowledge and wisdom.

Matt. 12:32 *And whosoever speaks a word against the Son of Man, it shall be forgiven him; but whosoever speaks against the Holy Spirit, it shall not be forgiven him, neither in this world, neither in the world to come.* If anyone is on the verge of committing a sin, the Holy Spirit is there to convict our hearts first, so if we proceed to commit, then there is no excuse that we are not informed.

Complete Reliance on God

Dan. 12:3 *And they that be **wise shall shine as the brightness of the firmament**, and they that turn many to righteousness as the stars forever and ever.* Trust in the Lord. If we are wise enough to recognize Jesus, the Messiah in His first advent, then we are fit in this event to "Shine as the Brightness of the Firmament". Then this corrupt world will see our favors from God, "that turn many to righteousness" and they can copy or emulate what we have done, and this I believe we did bear fruit. If we bear good fruit, then we please the God that loved us first, and we return with gratitude in our hearts: Love for the Lord Jesus. This is the Reward for the Righteous (those who believed in Jesus, made righteous by His Finished Work at the Cross).

Remember my brothers and friends in Faith; to be a True Christian is not hard to do, if we can truly believed. For Christ will always guide and encourage us.

Leave all your problems at the foot of Jesus, just like what Mary, the sister of Lazarus did at the foot of Jesus. Just stay close to Him and it is enough. We cannot do anything without Him. In true terms, Jesus cannot do anything also; without His Father in Heaven, Who sent Him.

Remember to: *Cast your burden upon the Lord (Jesus Christ), and He shall sustain you: He shall never suffer the righteous to be moved.* **Psalm 55:22**. Also Read Matt 11:28-30.

Definition of Faith

James 2:17 *Even so Faith, if it has not works, is dead being alone.* True Faith in Christ will produce good works, a faith that will bear good fruit. Therefore, the Holy Spirit here is telling us that good Faith and good works go hand in hand or they cannot be separate, or else it profits not God, nor man. Good works is the validation of your faith and proclaims your love for God.

James 2:26 *For as the body without the spirit is dead, so Faith without works is also dead.* Similarly the body of man without the spirit of God (When our spirit is possessed by Satan, it is dead, as told by God to Adam not to eat the fruit of the Tree of knowledge of good and evil) is dead, and so Faith without works is also dead. A spirit without Christ is dead and cannot bear good fruit and cannot become a **Member of the Body of Christ.**

Heb. 11:1 *Now Faith is the substance of things hoped for, the evidence of things not seen.* We have seen the billions of creation that are good and it abounds around and amongst us, but we have not seen the Creator, and so believing that there is a Creator is Faith indeed. The unseen Creator has proven His great works with evidence. That no one, cannot deny His presence among His people whom He has completely Blessed.

Heb. 11:2 *For by it the Elders obtained a good report.* This proclaims that our Patriarchs have done good things unto God to receive such approval. And also with us now in our generation must do good things unto God, to receive His approval.

If we receive God's approval, that means one thing. We have Faith in Him who created us, and He has given us the keys to His Kingdom for we are **Member of the Body of Christ.**

Heb. 11:3 *Through Faith we understand that the worlds were framed by the Word of God, so that things which are seen were not made of things which do appear.* Once we have Faith in the unseen Creator of things we see, it will be easy for us to understand His Words. Because we know that His Words are True and Holy. For He gives us wisdom, and guides us in our daily walk with Him to become **Members of the Body of Christ.** This also means we can thread on the spiritual realm as well as on the natural realm.

Heb. 11:6 *But without Faith it is impossible to please Him: for he who comes to God must believe that He is, and that He is a rewarder of them who diligently seek Him.* Only through Faith in Christ Jesus and Him Crucified: that we can please our Father God and be partakers of His riches. For our Father is our only source of all things we need and in our spiritual and mortal life. We can only consistently and diligent seek Father God if we are **Members of the Body of Christ.** For only in Him that our faith will not fail us even if Satan will desire to have us.

See Fig. 1: To understand what composes the **Body of Christ.**

CHAPTER 12

Forgive and Repent

A prayer: Psalm 51; To the Chief Musician (Lord Jesus), A psalm of David, when Nathan came to him, after he had gone in to Bathsheba. In this Chapter we will learn why it is important to repent and ask for forgiveness.

Psalm 51:1 *Have mercy upon me, O God, according to thy loving kindness: according unto the multitude of thy tender mercies blot out my transgressions.*

Psalm 51:3 *For I acknowledge my transgressions: and my sin ever before me.* Acceptance of sin or guilt is the number one prerequisite for the forgiveness of our sin, it is an act of humility by the sinner. David set aside his pride even though he is the king of Israel. It should be true for all of mankind as well. Read **Psalm 51:4**

Psalm 51:5 *Behold, I was shapen in iniquity; and in sin did my mother conceive me.* Confirms the fact that all men are sinners, by virtue on one man's sin, Adam. David admitted his sin and he humbled his self.

Psalm 51:6 *Behold, thou desirest truth in the inward parts: and in the hidden part thou shall make me to know wisdom.* David knows that God searches much deeper into his heart, and he asked for wisdom to know more about our Father.

Psalm 51:8 *Make me to hear joy and gladness; that the bones which thou hast broken may rejoice.* We are to be tested in fire.

Psalm 51:9 *Hide thy face from my sins, and blot out all mine iniquities.* David is pleading to God to forgive him of all his iniquities.

Psalm 51:10 *Create in me a clean heart, O God; and renew a right spirit within me.* A clean heart affords us humility that keeps us strong to reject temptation.

Psalm 51:11 *Cast me not away from thy presence; and take not thy holy spirit from me.* Lord, have mercy on us.

Psalm 51:12 *Restore unto me the joy of thy Salvation; and uphold me with thy free spirit.* Lord, set me free.

Psalm 51:13 *Then will I teach transgressors thy ways; and sinners will be converted unto thee.* I will declare your glory to the ends of the world and fulfill the Great Commission.

Psalm 51:14 *Deliver me from blood-guiltiness, O God, thou God of Salvation; and my tongue shall sing aloud of thy righteousness.* This is David's guilt in putting Uriah, the husband of Bathsheba, in great danger of dying. It was an act of committing murder. In this case, even though David is an anointed man by God still sometimes we give in to the temptation of Satan. This is proof that humans are weak. God knows we need grace.

David knows that his act is a sin, convicted by the Holy Spirit; still he pursued this evil act of conspiracy with his right hand man. This was not done by demons. It takes a king (Satan) to temp another king in the flesh. A big lesson for all men: that no one shall copy. Therefore the only remedy is to simply humble our hearts, repent and ask for forgiveness.

In return for God's forgiveness, David promised to tell all of God's Mercy, Justice and Righteousness.

Psalm 51:15 *O Lord, open thou my lips; and my mouth shall shew forth thy praise.* In repentance, the sinner almost always as a human instinct and tendency is to promise to give back as a show of remorse. This time King David, because he knows that he has offended the Lord that he must praise God.

Psalm 51:16 *For thou desirest not sacrifice; else would I give it: thou delightest not in burnt offering.* David acknowledges that the Lord desires worship more than anything else and he is willing to give all the types of offering that he knows, just to be forgiven by the Lord. This attitude is a very noble act of a remorseful man. The Holy Spirit is telling how a believer should act in case we commit a heinous crime and boasting is not the desired act. For it will not get us closer to our Lord.

Psalm 51:17 *The sacrifices of God are a broken spirit; a broken and a contrite heart, O God, thou wilt not despise.* This is also a prophecy of Christ at His Crucifixion. The Lamb of God is the ultimate sacrifice, and it is the only sacrifice acceptable to the Father in Heaven. No other sacrifice will matter; therefore men should not attempt to do another. All men must do is just accept in faith that Christ finished His work at the Cross.

Psalm 51:18 *Do good in thy pleasure unto Zion: build thou the walls of Jerusalem.* David's desire of his heart is to build the temple of God in Jerusalem.

Psalm 51:19 *Then shalt thou be pleased with the sacrifices of righteousness, with burnt offering and whole burnt offering: then shall they offer bullocks upon thine altar.* In the Old Testament time, burnt offering sacrifices is acceptable to God, but God knows only the perfect sacrifice of His son Jesus at the cross will atone for the sins of mankind.

David's act of repentance is our template on how to repent our sins. It begins from our contrite heart.

Forgiveness:

Matt. 6:14 *For if you forgive men their trespasses, your Heavenly Father will also forgive you.* This specifies one of the requirements to enter into the Kingdom of God.

Matt. 6:15 *But if you forgive not men their trespasses, neither will your Father forgive your trespasses.* The above 2 verses, tells all of us that it is imperative to forgive our fellow man's trespass against us. For our Heavenly Father, (our spiritual Father) will not forgive our sins either. To be forgiven is essential for us, so we can become **Members of the Body of Christ.**

There is no place for hate to exist in His Kingdom. The same reason we are admonished to love one another as Christ have loved us unconditionally.

Thus Christ requires all to forgive. For forgiveness is result of the Atoning Work of Christ at the cross. All of us is a beneficiary of this Atoning Work if we will only acknowledge Christ as the Son of God and He purchased our debt by His shed blood on that rugged Cross.

CHAPTER 13

Jesus Christ of the Bible

To really seek the Kingdom of God,
and his righteousness; we must know who He
Is. Let us begin in the Old Testament

Who is Jesus Christ?

John 14:6 *I am the Way, the Truth, and the Life: no man comes unto the Father, but by Me.*

Jesus Preparing for His First Advent
Jesus is The Way: (The Sacrificial Lamb)

God's Commandment to Abraham: In Gen. 22:2, *And He said, Take now your son, your only son Isaac, whom you love, and go into the land of Moriah; and offer him there for a Burnt Offering upon one of the mountains which I will tell you of.* Please read also Gen. 22:3-9 to have a complete background of the story;

Gen. 22:10 *And Abraham stretch forth his hand and took the knife to slay his son.* This act of Abraham validates his faith to the Father.

His works: that made him holy and perfect in the eyes of God. Our perfect example on how to validate our Faith with good works is Abraham. Of course none of us can duplicate what he did, but we can do one of the other trillion ways to show we love the Lord Jesus. I advise believers not to worry on how to please God, we just open our hearts to Him so the Lord Jesus can call dwell and call us His temple, and He will tell us what to do to please Him. Remember Buck Owens song: Act Naturally? Just like that. There is no need to labor. Just remember Christ every day and give thanks. And He will be with us. The prophets call Him Emmanuel.

Gen. 22:12 *And He said lay not your hand upon the lad, neither do you anything unto him: for now I know that you fear God, seeing you have not withheld your son, your only son from me.* Abraham acted the way God expects His creation to do, that we must fear and obey Him. It was exactly a way of God's will. The Father God has shown us the manner or way, a clue of how He will claim us back, from our bondage to Satan. It will involve a sacrificial system being pre-pictured in Isaac as the Burnt Offering to pay a ransom. Until the appointed time comes, it will be Jesus. In the same way, Our Father in Heaven will not withhold His Son Jesus for our sake, to provide a way for the salvation of man.

Indeed, It is **Jesus Christ as the unblemished Sacrificial Lamb on the Cross at Calvary**, some 2000 years ago; At the Feast of Passover. Prophecy was fulfilled.

Abrahamic Covenant

Gen. 12:2 *And I will make you a great Nation, and I will bless you, and make your name great; and you shall be a blessing.*

Gen. 12:3 *I will bless them who bless you; and curse him who curses you: and in you shall all families of the earth be blessed.* As of this writing, I can see that God is blessing those: that blesses the seed of Abraham and cursing those that cursed. It is very obvious in the Middle East. God kept His promise. It is a very re-assuring feeling to know our God will never fail us.

Truly our God, the God of Abraham, Isaac and Jacob is a great God.

The Tree of Life:

Gen. 2:9. *The Tree of Life is also in the midst of the Garden.* If Adam and Eve ate the fruit of this tree first, I believe, they would surely lived forever (eternal life) with God. None of these problems that man suffer now will we ever endure. This Tree resembles and pre-pictures Jesus Christ himself.

The Tree of Knowledge of Good and Evil:

Eph. 2:16 *And that He* (Jesus Christ) *might reconcile both unto God in one body by the Cross, having slain the enmity thereby.* This tree represents the Cross, it is the tree of death, trials, sufferings and tribulations, because Satan is part of that tree.

With Christ hanging on the cross, Satan has to move away and with the tree being made holy by Christ, nullified the bondage of man to Satan. By the Finished Work of Christ at the Cross: now man can be reconciled with God and there is no barrier that separates Creator and creation. Christ' crucifixion being the means, salvation from sin is now attainable simply though Faith.

Please note that at the temple, the veil of the Holy of Holies that signifies separation of God and man was rent from top to bottom during Christ crucifixion.

Matt. 16:24 *Then said Jesus unto His Disciples. If any man will come after Me, let Him deny himself, and take up his cross and follow Me.* To accept the fact that man cannot do the things of God (spiritual) by him alone, but rather to rely solely on God for everything we need and do.

The Living Water

At the Bitter Waters of Marah: Ex. 15:23 *And when they came to Marah, they could not drink of the waters of Marah, for they were bitter: therefore the name of it was Marah.*

Ex. 15:25 *And he cried unto the Lord; and the Lord showed him a Tree; which when he had cast into the waters, the waters were made sweet: there He made for them a Statute and an Ordinance, and there He proved them.* The Tree here is also symbolizes Jesus Christ himself crucified. He can make Living Water out of bitter water. The tree can transform the bitter water into sweet water. Jesus can transform the water into wine, in a wedding at Cana. The tree also symbolizes the Cross and Jesus Christ is the trunk and the horizontal arms or branches, are the believers or church that will bear fruit. We bear fruit if we finish the work given us by God's will.

The Jewish Roots

The Patriarchs: Abraham, Isaac and Jacob (Israel); are installed by Father God as symbolic roots drawing the provisions to branches from Him, the Father. For the Father God is the Source of all our provisions, whether they are spiritual or material needs. Therefore make no mistake that we acquire our health and wealth solely on our own efforts. We have to recognize the truth that God has to be our partner in all our lives, whether in flesh or in spirit.

The Covenant Confirmed

Gen. 22:15 *And the Angel of the Lord called unto Abraham out of Heaven the second time,*

Gen. 16 *And said by myself have I sworn, says the Lord, for because you have done this thing, and have not withheld your son, your only son:* Although Isaac was not sacrificed in the flesh, but in the spirit, he was, and he was also raised from the dead. In essence **Isaac was a type of Christ.**

Gen. 22:17 *That in blessing I will bless you, and in multiplying I will multiply your seed as the stars of the heaven and as the sand; which is upon the sea shore; and your seed shall possess the gates of his enemies.* "Seed" pertains to the **Members Body of Jesus Christ.** This includes the Church and for all people of all time who had acknowledged the true and only one God. The "gates of his enemies" speaks of Christ defeating Satan in His first Advent and removed his spiritual right to hold man in sin. Simply called Redemption. UK and USA are the seed of Abraham and controls the commercial maritime and military uses of the sea.

Gen. 22:18 *And, your seed shall all the nations of the Earth be blessed; because you have obeyed My Voice.* Obedience to the

Word of God is required, and Faith in Christ must be present in man's spiritual wellbeing to have obedience.

Jesus Christ, (Melchizedek) High Priest

Gen. 14:18 *Melchizedek, king of Salem brought forth bread and wine: and he was the Priest of the Most High God.*

Gen. 14:19 *And he blessed him* (Abraham*), and said, Blessed be Abram of the Most High God. Possessor of Heaven and Earth.*

Gen. 14:20 *And blessed be the Most High God, Who has delivered your enemies unto your hand. And he gave him tithes of all.* Bible scholars believed that Melchizedek is Shem, the son of Noah. (The word Semite comes from the name Shem).

Heb. 6:19 *Which hope we have as an anchor of the soul, both sure and steadfast, and which enters into that within the Veil.* Jesus entered into the Holy of Holies on our behalf. He could do it because He is without sin.

Heb. 6:20 *Whither the forerunner is for us entered, even Jesus, made an High Priest for ever after the order of Melchizedek.* The Priesthood order of Melchizedek was ahead and without end compared to the Priesthood order of Aaron and the Pharisees, which are to end at the First Advent of Christ. Christ is now our High Priest forever.

The titles of Melchizedek: King of Salem, Priest of the Most High, King of Righteousness, King of Peace or Prince of Peace. All of these are also the titles of Jesus Christ.

Jesus Christ, The Servant

Joseph, Son of Jacob (Israel); He was sold for 20 pieces of silver. He was accused of wrong- doing, he did not do. He did not come to condemn, but to save his brethren. He prophesied and interpret; the word of God. He was with God, Emanuel (Jesus).

Joseph is the more complete pre-picture of who Jesus Christ is. For he was a servant, he suffered stripes in prison, he was accused wrongly, he was provider to his brethren in time of famine, he was taken from his family to become a slave, he was sold for 20 pieces of silver (the price of a slave in his time), he fulfilled prophecies, He has the favor of God.

Jesus Christ, The Ministry

Gen. 41:46 *And Joseph was 30 years old when he stood before Pharaoh king of Egypt. And Joseph went throughout all the land of Egypt.* Joseph was appointed Governor, of all Egypt by Pharaoh. And all of Egypt must obey him. He was second to Pharaoh in power. Similarly, Our Lord Jesus Christ was 30 years old when He began His ministry with at a wedding in Cana of Galilee, He did His first miracle by transforming water into the best wine ever. **John 2:7-8**

Jesus Christ, The Provider

Joseph; Gen 42:25 *Then Joseph commanded to fill their sacks with corn, and to restore every man's money into his sack, and to give them provision for the way: and thus he did unto them.* Jesus is also our Provider thru Him. He is our Jehovah Jireh.

Jesus Christ, The Deliverer and Law Giver

Moses: Ex. 13:3 *And Moses said unto the people, Remember this day, in which you came out of Egypt, out of the house of bondage; for by strength of Hand of the Lord brought you out of this place: there shall no leaven bread to be eaten.*

Ex. 13:4 *This day came ye out in the month of Abib.* Moses, in the likeness to Jesus is also a deliverer. They both delivered us from bondage.

Moses received the 10 Commandments (we call the Law) from Father God and gave it to the Jews to follow. More commandments were given plus rituals and sacrifices that must be followed. All in all, the Laws totaled 613. No man could do all these, except God-man Jesus Christ.

King David, The Warrior and Conqueror

King David was Chosen as King and the Anointed:

1 Sam. 16:12 *And he sent, and brought him in. Now he was ruddy, and withal of a beautiful countenance, and goodly to look to. And the Lord said, Arise, anoint him: for this is he.*

1 Sam. 16:13 *Then Samuel took the horn of oil, and anoint him in the midst of his brethren: and the spirit of the Lord came upon David from that day forward,*

King David has fought many wars and won them all. He consolidated the Kingdom of Israel in terms of land area and possession. He is also considered by many Jews; as the father of Jesus Christ (they call Jesus as Son of David). In my view David is also a type of Christ in all the things that he had achieved for the Glory of God. King David pre-pictured Jesus Christ in His Second Coming wherein He will be a Conquering Warrior by defeating all His enemies at the Battle of Armageddon.

King Solomon, The Temple Builder

King Solomon, Son of David: David's oath to Bath-sheba: **1Kings 1:29** *And the king swore, and said, As the Lord lives. Who has redeemed my soul out of all distress.*

By David swear. It shows that there is power and authority vested in him by the Lord God to proclaim his son Solomon as the next king of Israel.

**1 Kings 1:*30* *Even as I swore unto you* (Bath-sheba) *by the Lord God of Israel, saying. Assuredly Solomon your son shall reign after me, and he sit upon my throne in my stead, even so will I certainly do this day.*

1 Kings 1: 39 *And Zadok the Priest took an horn of oil out of the Tabernacle, and anointed Solomon, And they blew the trumpet; and all the people said, God save king Solomon.* Now Solomon confirmed as King of Israel. Solomon is a type of Christ, as he built the Jewish Temple.

Solomon Asked for Wisdom:

1 Kings 3:3 *And Solomon loved the Lord, walking in the statutes of David his father: only he sacrificed and burnt incense in high places.*

1 Kings 3:4 *And the king went to Gibeon to sacrifice there; for that was the great high place: a thousand burnt offerings did Solomon offer upon that Altar.* At Gibeon is where Moses built a Tabernacle for it was the highest place in that part of the world at the time.

1 Kings 3:5 *In Gibeon the Lord appeared to Solomon in a dream by night: and God said, Ask what shall I give you.*

1 Kings 3:9 *Give therefore your servant an understanding heart to judge Your people, that I may discern between good and bad: for who is able to judge this Your so great a people?* In short, Solomon asked for wisdom.

1 Kings 3:11 *And God said unto him, because you have asked this thing, and have not asked yourself long life; neither have asked riches for yourself, nor have asked the life of your enemies; but have asked for yourself understanding to discern judgment;*

When God ask King Solomon in a dream, what does he want? He replied he wants understanding to discern judgment. God was pleased and gave him everything. This event also pre-pictures King Solomon as a type of Christ. What he did was a representation of the characteristic of Jesus Christ.

If we must observe and analyze, all the events and persons previously mentioned, we can summarize that they are leading us to the last Passover of Jesus Christ at Calvary. He is the unblemished Lamb of God. The Jewish people have sacrificed millions of bullocks and goats, but none was able to atone for theirs and our sins.

Solomon Builds the Temple:

1 Kings 6:1 *And it came to pass in the four hundred and eightieth year after the Children of Israel were come out of the land of Egypt, in the fourth year of Solomon's reign over Israel, in the month of Zif, which is the second month that he began to build the House of the Lord.*

1 Kings 6:19 *And the Oracle he prepared in the house within, to set the Ark of the Covenant of the Lord.*

John 2:19 *Jesus answered and said unto them, Destroy this Temple, in 3 days I raise it up.* Jesus spoke of the Temple of His Body and builds it in the hearts of believers or Church.

The Ark of the Covenant:

The Ark of the Covenant personifies Jesus Christ. It is a type of Throne of God. I believe it is a replica of what is the Throne of God in Heaven.

God commanded Moses to construct the Ark while they were camped at Mt Sinai during the Jews 40 years wandering in the desert or wilderness. Read Ex. 25:10-22; 37:1-9. The Ark is constructed from Shittim Wood, referred as indestructible wood and a type of Perfect, unblemished physical Body of Christ Jesus.

111

Ex. 25:10 *And they shall make an Ark of Shittim Wood: two cubits and a half shall be the length thereof, and a cubit and a half the breath thereof, and a cubit and a half the height thereof.*

Ex. 25:22 *And there I will meet you, and I will commune with you from above the Mercy Seat, from between the two Cherubims which are upon the Ark of the Testimony, of all things which I will give you in Commandments unto the Children of Israel.* This verse validates that the Ark is used by God to interact with the Israelites. And the Ark goes wherever the Israelites go and it has helped them win battles. The First Temple built by King Solomon housed the Ark for over 400 years. The Babylonians destroyed the Temple in around 586 BC, and then the Ark disappeared. Until now the Ark is nowhere to be found.

Upon the Israelites return from Medo-Persian captivity, they rebuilt the Temple on the same location. And without the Ark, they built the Holy of Holies. Once a year a Holy man of Israel, usually the Chief Pharisee will enter the Holy of Holies to make offering unto the Lord for all their sins.

At Christ crucifixion: in **Matt. 27:51** *And, behold, the veil of the temple was rent in twain from the top to the bottom; and the earth did quake, and the rocks rent;* The veil of Holy of Holies was torn apart from top to bottom to signify that there is a new way for man to interact with God Almighty. It is through Jesus.

The Holy of Hollies located at the Second Temple represents as the Ark of the Covenant.

By the same token, in today's world, God the Father interacts with His Children through His Son Jesus Christ. Through Christ we receive God's love, and blessings of all things that we, the believers' need.

I believe in today's world, the Holy of Hollies or the Ark of the Covenant is the **Body of Christ.**

At this moment no one in the natural world can ever see or find the Ark. I believe, it was converted back to spiritual object and it is now in Paradise. There is no need for man to see the Ark physically bad people might use its powers for bad reasons.

Jesus Christ, Our Shepherd!

Psalm 23, a Psalm of David: The Shepherd

Psalm 23:1 *The Lord is My Shepherd; I shall not want,* In this verse, David understand the experience of being with God and declares that, the Shepherd is Jesus Christ as Lord and he will never need any other as Lord, because Christ is the one and only. And if Christ is the one and only Lord for King David, then it must be the same for you and me. No other God.

Psalm 23:2 *He makes me to lie down in green pastures: He leads Me beside the still waters,* If the Lord is our Shepherd, His blessings are provided in abundance and He gives us spiritual peace and assurance of Salvation.

Psalm 23:3 *He restores my soul; He leads me in the paths of Righteousness for His name's sake.* He gives us rest, the Sabbath and by His grace and mercy, He makes us without sin and forgave our sins not to be remembered no more. In other words we are righteous in the eyes of our Father in Heaven, and His commandments are our paths or our ways to righteousness. Only if we are with Him, then we can fulfill His edicts.

Psalm 23:4 *Yes, though I walk through the valley of the shadow of death, I will fear no evil: for you are with me; Your rod and your staff they comfort me.* In this world, we dwell in the valley of death, and in the valley of graven images, where the ways are ways of evil, but we should not fear them; for we wear the armors of God. Christ Jesus gives us all the protection we need and comfort to have no worries or fear. To put exactly where we are daily, we are in the **Body of Christ**. After death in the flesh, we are then sanctified and become permanent members.

Psalm 23:5 *You prepare a table before me in the presence of mine enemies: thou anointest my head with oil; my cup runneth over.* Our enemies are the principalities of evil and Jesus prepared a dwelling place for us in this Earth and also provided protection through the Holy Spirit.

Here, God puts us on a pedestal and makes us kings over our enemies and our blessings are in abundance beyond compare. This place is **Paradise.**

This is one of the privileges of being a **Member of the Body of Christ;** we have access to **Paradise.**

Psalm 23:6 *Surely goodness and mercy shall follow me all the days of my life: and I will dwell in the house of the Lord forever.* We have eternal life only through Christ. If we are good in the sight of our Father, we have the assurance that God's grace and mercy are unto us forever; for we are **Members of the Body of Christ**, The Holy Child Jesus (Santo Nino de Cebu, the Holy Child of Prague and Santo Nino de Atocha are the same, only they are in different location.)

Similarly on Earth, imagine you are a member of a Family that loves you, you have all the privilege of eating whatever food there is in the fridge, you can drive whatever car the family owns, as long as your good behavior and allegiance remains with the family. With our Father in Heaven, the God Family system is the same.

CHAPTER 14

The Holy Days of God

These **8 Holy Days of God** are the Believer's guide to determine where his position is, with respect to his relationship with our Father and Christ Jesus. And the fulfillment of God's major events revealed through Jesus Christ our Lord. With it are 8 mysteries that a Believer must try to unlock and understand. Even Bible scholars have failed to fully unlock and understand. In this book, we will discuss it, based on revelation by the Holy Spirit. No man, I believe can do it on his own. Four of these Feast; have been fulfilled on appointed time and all are revealed through Christ.

Therefore the remaining 4 will surely be fulfilled on God's time. No one knows except the Father, even Jesus does not know.

Our Lord God has commanded Moses to tell the Jews during their 40 years of wandering in the wilderness to obey to celebrate and observe these Feast every year without fail. Today, most Jews of Israel are still doing it without fail.

Moses was told: **Lev. 23:2** *Speak unto the children of Israel, and say unto them. Concerning the Feast of the Lord, which you shall proclaim to be holy convocations, even these are my Feast.*

Day of Passover:

Lev. 23:5 *In the fourteenth day of the first month at evening is the Lord's Passover.* In the Old Testament, the Jewish people are required by God to celebrate and remember the day when the Angel of the Lord passed over their dwellings in Egypt where they painted it with blood of the sacrificed unblemished lamb. All those who obeyed, their first-born sons were spared and survived the plague. While those who did not, their first-born sons died including the son of Pharaoh with no exceptions in Egypt, I believe. The Jews were commanded to observed and re-enact the Passover every year. They were doing it until Christ came to the cross. For what reason? I believe the celebration is a pre-picture, that in the fullness of time a shedding of the blood event will fulfill the redemption of man.

Before the beginning of the New Testament, this Feast will culminate in Jesus hanging with His arms and hands spread out nailed to the cross. He will suffer and die to shed His blood. It figures as Redemption of man's indebtedness to sin. The Cross of Calvary being the means to achieve the Finished Work of Christ. In the Christian World: This Feast is the only one we celebrate and offer reverence in this day and age. We call the Holy Week.

In this Church Age, the Bible does not command us to celebrate or not celebrate Passover. What we are commanded to do is the breaking of the bread that it is His body and we must eat it as often as we can to remember Him and proclaim His death until He comes again. This is so, because the shedding of the blood of Christ will not happen again. He said while hanging on the cross: It is finished. We should not look forward to it, rather we must wait for His Second Coming.

Why does Christ have to die on the Cross? Why not by any other means?

In **Gen. 2:8** *And God planted a Garden eastward in Eden (Paradise)...* **9** *... the Tree of Life also in the midst of the Garden and the Tree of Knowledge of Good and Evil.*

The Tree of Life represents Christ and the Tree of Knowledge of Good and Evil represents Satan and Man. Man is the Good and Satan is the Evil. That is why the Lord commanded Adam not to eat of the fruit of the tree, because it contains Evil. Adam has complete information that is why the Scriptures say he was not deceived. Only Eve was deceived.

Picture a man with his arms stretch out he looks like a cross. The wooden cross: represent man and Satan, which mean suffering, pain, sorrows, problems and troubles. Now in God' s economy, He will only redeem man if He sends His own son to remove evil in this world by the shedding of blood of Christ on the cross. You see, anything that Christ touches becomes holy or whole. He heals by just touching the sick. In the same way, when He was crucified on the cross, He defeated Satan. He made that cross holy. A cross without Christ is nothing. When we see a Cross erected without Christ in it, it means nothing. The means for our redemption is Christ hanging on the Cross. Therefore the Tree of Knowledge of Good and Evil has to be removed from this Earth, and Christ has done it.

Today: as **Members of the Body of Christ** when we go to Paradise or Eden we will not find the Tree of Knowledge of Good and Evil, what we will find is the Tree of Life, Jesus Christ. But in this world, the place of the sinners and wicked, here we find the Tree of Knowledge of Good and Evil. At Christ Second Coming He will deal with Evil and remove this tree as well on Earth to establish His Kingdom on Earth.

Feast of Unleavened Bread

Lev. 23:6 *And on the fifteenth day of the same month is the Feast of Unleavened Bread unto the Lord, seven days you must eat Unleavened Bread*

Lev. 23:7 *In the first day you shall have an holy convocation: you shall do no servile work therein.*

Lev. 23:8 *But you shall offer an Offering made by fire unto the Lord seven days: in the seventh day is an holy convocation: you shall do no servile work.* In the Old Testament, the Jewish people are required to celebrate or observe this Feast to cleanse their body of their sins but eating unleavened bread for seven days. 7 days signifies perfection.

In the New Testament: The Unleavened Bread signifies the perfect and unblemished Body of Christ in His First Advent pointing to Christ's Last Supper with His Disciples. This was highlighted by: the breaking of the bread and drinking of the wine. His Body is composed of the **Holy Spirit and the Spirit and flesh of a Woman in Virgin Mary.** By virtue of conception and Virgin Birth, the Son of God was made flesh. And His Body was broken at His Crucifixion. **This Feast requires a First Fruit Offering** and it is the first of 3 Feast that requires. Similarly Jesus is a First Fruit. He is also called Fruit of the Womb. This Feast also indicates 30 fold blessings. The men coming to this Feast shall not come empty handed, starts on a Sabbath after the crucifixion of Christ.

Feast of the FIRSTFRUITS:

Lev. 23:10 *Moses: Speak unto the Children of Israel, and say unto them, When you come into the land which I give unto you, and shall reap the harvest thereof, then you shall bring a sheaf of the firstfruits of your harvest unto the Priest;*

Lev. 23:11 *And he shall wave the sheaf before the Lord, to be accepted for you: on the morrow after the Sabbath the Priest shall wave it.* In the New Testament: The Feast of First Fruit represents the Resurrection of our Lord Jesus Christ

Lev. 23:12 *And you shall offer that day when you wave the sheaf an he lamb without blemish of the first year for a burnt Offering unto the Lord.* This Feast is celebrated on a Sunday, a day after the second Sabbath after Christ crucifixion.

Feast of PENTECOST or Feast of WEEKS:

First Fruit offering is required. The males will not come empty handed. This Feast also requires First fruits Offerings:

Lev. 23:15; *And you shall count unto you from the morrow after Sabbath; from the day you brought the sheaf of the Wave Offering; seven Sabbaths shall be complete:* Forty nine days complete plus 1 day is fifty (day of celebration, observance, or commemoration; Hence, the name "Pentecost".

Lev. 15:16 *Even unto the morrow after the seventh Sabbath shall you number fifty days; and you shall offer; a new meat offering unto the Lord.* ("new meat" are newly harvested grains)

Lev 23:17 *You shall bring out of you habituations two wave loaves of two tenth deals: as they shall be of fine flour; they shall be baked with leaven; they are the Firstfruits unto the Lord.* Along with this Bread Offering that pre-figure the Body of Christ, which He gave up for man in His first advent are the Burnt Offering of seven unblemished lambs, and one kid of goat for Sin Offering and two – one year old lambs for Peace Offerings. To the Jews of the Old Testament, they were not told what is this Feast for. They just have to do it.

In the New Testament: These three meat offerings; pre-figures the redemption process that will finally happen on the Cross of Calvary. These rituals; was fulfilled exactly fifty days after the Crucifixion of Christ. The outpouring of the Holy Spirit happened on this Pentecost, Day of the Lord. Although the Holy Spirit is now present on earth, and can dwell in the hearts of every living believer, but the flesh remained corrupt (naked) ("*baked with leaven*").

The purpose of Holy Spirit coming down is to perform Spiritual Baptism or we can say circumcision of the heart on every believer.

Thus allowing the Church to suppress temptation (thus avoiding to commit sin) by the power of Jesus living in him, making him the temple of God.

To further articulate: while we are still in this body of flesh as a Church we are declared **Members of the Body of Christ.** In this position we can receive all the Divine Privileges as the Son of God. Yes, although we still have the sin and corrupt nature, we can still backslide in faith and risk to lose our membership. That is why we have to do the communion ritual: the eating of the broken bread and drinking the wine to constantly remind us that to be in the Body of Christ is truly imperative. Take heart, our corrupt nature will be shed away when we reach our final milestone of first death, which should be joyful, peaceful and painless.

The Holy Spirit sanctifies the believer. This also indicates 60 fold blessings.

The Feast of the TRUMPETS

Lev 23:24 *Speak unto the Children of Israel, saying in the seventh month, in the first day of the month, shall you have a Sabbath, a memorial of blowing of trumpets, an holy convocation.* (I believed this is a High Sabbath, it may not fall on the seventh day) The only Feast of the Lord celebrated on a new moon.

Lev. 23:25 *You shall do no servile work therein, but you shall offer an Offering made by fire unto the Lord.* In the New Testament: This Feast pertains to the Rupture of the Church, signifying the end of the Church Age, meaning the last man spirit that accepted Jesus Christ as Lord and Savior is grafted into the Vine that completes the **Members of the Body of Christ.** At this point in time, the 7 trumpets will sound and the Rupture of the Church takes place. Plagues and wars will follow. The plagues are human suffering highlighted by the 7 years Great Tribulations. This will end at the Battle of Armageddon. See **1 Cor. 15:51-54**

As a Christian, am I supposed to observe, commemorate or celebrate the Feast of the Trumpets? I believe so. In the Church Age, Christians are considered the Israel of God. The celebration might not be as lavish, a prayer or convocation will suffice because the Temple of God is now our hearts and body.

Why? Because the Christians/believers/followers of Christ are the ones grafted into the True Vine now. **See John 15:1-12.**

The Jews has been withered and cut off, because they **did not accept Christ as their Messiah in His first Advent.**

How and where will I go to make offering and celebrate this Feast of the Lord?

That is my problem too. Since; there are no more Temples to do it, as it was destroyed; by the Romans in 70 AD. There are no Churches or House of Prayer doing to commemorate these Feasts. Check out Larry and Tiz Huch Ministry in Dallas, TX; they may be doing it.

This is my alternative: As for me, I will be doing it with a communion at a local Catholic Church so I could remember, or celebrate, or observe these Feasts the best way I can. Because the local Catholic Churches are doing the breaking of the Bread and

Drinking the Wine at every mass they celebrate. As what I have done in the past two years with the Feast of Unleavened Bread, Feast of Pentecost, and Feast of Tabernacles. This April 2014 I will be completing my second cycle. I have to do these offering in remembrance of Him, Jesus Christ as he has commanded us at His Last Supper. Just like everybody else, the local church, I am going to, do not take the effort to even discuss these Feasts. Many Christians of today are very ignorant of these Feasts of the Lord.

Deut. 16:16 *Three times in a year you shall all your males appear before the Lord your God in the place which He shall chose, in the Feast of Unleavened Bread* (April), *and in the Feast of Weeks* (Pentecost, the first days of June, a Sunday), *and in the Feast of Tabernacles* (September or October): *and they shall not appear before the LORD empty.*

Deut. 16:17 *Every man shall give as he is able, according to the Blessing of the LORD your God which He has given you.* To receive the blessings we must know how to give to the Lord. King Solomon is our example.

Some Pastors are saying that observance of these Holy Days of God; will bring unlimited blessings in today's world. I would believe so, for God loves us more when we remember Him and there is nothing impossible with Him. God will open the floodgates of Heaven to bless us.

I have a testimony to tell you. In the past 2 years I remember, I have read this verse Deut 16:16 so many times and I memorized it. I have been comparing it with Mark 4:20. As I recall, included in this verse are the numbers 30, 60 and 100 fold. But now, in my astonishment, I don't find them anymore. I have looked at almost all the Bible that my hands can get to. Is it that I am older now and my memory is failing me? I really wonder as I am writing this book now.

The Day of Atonement:

Lev. 23:27 *Also on the tenth day of the seventh month there shall be a day of Atonement: it shall be an holy convocation unto you; and you shall afflict your soul* (commandment to fast), *and offer an Offering made by fire unto the LORD.* "Offering made by fire Unto the Lord" means a celebration with food that we do with our Lord and Savior. (A Communion with God.) I can imagine we make our God and all the saints and angels happy. This Feast is an event that will take place after the Battle of Armageddon and Satan is defeated and bound and sent to the bottomless pit at the center of the Earth. So he cannot promote his evil ways for a thousand years.

Lev. 23:28 *And you shall do no work in that same day: for it is a day of Atonement, to make an atonement, for you before the Lord your God.*

I quote "(This is the one day; of the year that the High Priest went into the Holy of Holies to offer up incense, and blood on the Mercy Seat, all for himself and the entirety of Israel; from Expositors' Study Bible, by Jimmy Swaggart Ministries)."

In the New Testament: The Atonement of the Church plus: all the human souls who returned to God; survived the seven years Great Tribulation. The Jews will be grafted back into the True VINE and will be together with the Christians in the **Body of Christ**.

This will come to pass, I believe after the Battle of Armageddon and the Bible prophecy is fulfilled.

The Holy Bible says that it is now appointed unto man once to die. On this first death, the Church/believer will shed away his corrupt flesh/body. Then and only then that the believer can be atoned for. Feast of Atonement: The old corrupted body will be replaced with a glorified one. Sin does not have any place in the Kingdom of God.

Jesus will clothe us spiritually, providing us with a glorified body. We will never be naked again in the eyes of God. It will be the same human body before the fall of Adam to sin.

Feast of the Tabernacles:

This is the third Feast that requires First Fruits Offering unto the Lord:

Lev. 23:34 *Speak unto the Children of Israel, saying, The fifteenth day of this seventh month shall be the Feast of Tabernacles for seven days unto the Lord.*

Lev. 23:35 *On the first day shall be an holy convocation; you shall do no servile work therein*

Lev. 23:36 *Seven days you shall offer an Offering made by fire unto the Lord:* **on the eight day** *shall be an holy convocation unto you; and you shall offer an Offering made by fire unto the Lord; it is a solemn assembly; and you shall do no servile work therein.* This Feast event will come to pass after the Feast of Atonement; the Church and all believers (saved souls) will be gathered and placed in a

Booth to be waiting for their King Jesus Christ. They are totally protected inside the booth or tabernacles and all those inside are looking up expectantly. This Feast also indicates hundred fold blessings.

This is also the coming down of the New Jerusalem or New Heaven.

Feast of the Last Great Day

"on the eight day" I will considered it as the **Feast of the Last Great Day**; I believe this is the Wedding: Between the Bridegroom (Jesus) and the Bride (Church) after these events come to pass; the Millennial Kingdom Age will start.

These Feasts gives us a chronology of events that will all come to pass according to God's appointed time, it will be our markers, where we are, our position, and our relationship with Jesus. It will give us our defining moment. Spiritually. If you are aware of exactly where you are, then you can be rest assured where you are going.

The Feast of Passover, Feast of Unleavened Bread, The Feast of First Fruits and the Feast of Pentecost had all come to pass; therefore the next 4 remaining Feast will surely come to pass.

Check this out: The last Feast that came to pass was the Feast of Pentecost exactly 50 days after the Feast of Passover, now the next will be the Feast of the Trumpets, if we will look at the Jewish Calendar, the Feast of Trumpets is about 3.5 months after Pentecost on a calendar year, and it's now about 2000 years after Pentecost and the Feast of Trumpets has not come to pass yet, I believe that this next Feast of Trumpets is still about a millennium and a half away. It is contrary to what many Bible scholars predicted.

Jesus Christ's ministry and first miracle began at a wedding at Cana of Galilee and will culminate also at a Wedding in His Second Coming.

It is important to discuss and understand the 8 Feast of God or 8 Holy days of God. Not in a legalistic point of view, but rather to accept it as a guide to all who believes in God, where God wants us to be. Now if we look closely what had transpired, it brings the believer unto the **Kingdom of God**. Where would we want to be?

Parable of the Sower:

Mark 4:3 *Hearken, Behold, there went out a sower to sow.*

Mark 4:4 *And it came to pass, as He sowed, some fell by the wayside, and the fowls of the air came and devoured them up.* "seeds" refers to Gospel of Christ, "wayside" refers to people who don't care much about their **spiritual wellbeing** and does not want to learn about the holy ways of God because they were not exposed to it or the Gospel was not learned yet. "fowls of the air" refers to Satan and his demons powers and emissaries: **Read Eph 2:2**. I believe this is due to the Theory of Evolution being taught in all Public schools instead of Creation model, despite the fact that it remains to be a theory with no scientific substantiation. With the sad irony: Public Schools receive funding from the Church. Talking about biting the hands that feeds. The Creation model to its credit has proven itself beyond evidence after evidence, which is fact. While a few atheist and unbelievers, who managed the Department of Education has twisted the Word of God. This flawed system led many will be deceived, it also resulting in chaos in schools where numerous killing spree happened in the last 30 years. They have no answers why it is happening. The whole country does not know either because most of us are not a thinking person.

Mark 4:5 *And some fell on stony ground, where it had not much earth, and immediately it sprung up, because it had no depth of earth;*

Mark 4:6 *But when the sun was up, it was scorched; and because it had no root, it withered away.* "stony ground" refers to people with hardened heart, they might accept the Gospel for a while without commitment and their faith dies not giving importance to spiritual wellness.

Mark 4:7 *And some fell among thorns, and thorns grew up, and choke it, and yielded no fruit.* Refers to people who receives the Gospel in good faith but mingle with someone who gives bad spiritual influence and finally goes back to earthly ways again and backslides.

Mark 4:8 *And other fell on good ground, and did yield fruit that sprang up and increased; and brought forth, some thirty, some sixty, and some an hundred.*

Mark 4:9 *And He said unto them. He who has the ears to hear, let him hear.* "on good ground" are those who believed and accepted the Gospel of Christ and had brought forth fruit.

But some thirty means that the cares of this world still gets to them somehow; symbolically, they were able to get out of Egypt, but just wandered in the wilderness, still have some doubts about their faith in God. We call them people of little faith. These people are those who died in the wilderness. Sadly did not even get to see the Promise Land.

Some sixty would mean people of good faith but has not gone all the way in denying themselves of this world, but we can say they have seen the Promise Land, but was not able to go into it and have not experienced what is it like to live a life overflowing with milk and honey. Just like Moses.

Some hundred fold, a faith that has not wavered, it is an all-in faith being so steadfast even in death will not deny his love for the Lord Jesus. A Christian position a believer must aim for. It represents unlimited love blessings from God. And you also dispense that love even to the unlovely. It is this faith that bears so much fruit. A God like love is manifested in the believer. These are the Joshuas and Calebs who were able to reach the Promise Land.

The land where there is unlimited flow of milk and honey (unlimited provision courtesy of our Father in Heaven).

The good ground who bears fruit, are the **Members of the Body of Christ.** They are grafted to the True Vine, thereby they receive all the blessings they ask for (food/nutrients) from the Father. See Fig. 1.

Summary of the 8 Holy Days of God:

The Chronological Progression of Our Faith:

1. We begin our journey of Faith in God by acknowledgement of the Messiah Christ, the only begotten Son of our Father. At the **Day of Passover,** the Finished Work of Christ at the Cross of Calvary and Resurrection from death has defeated Satan. Now our debt and bondage to sin is fully paid for. The moment we confess with our mouth that we accept Christ as Lord and Savior, and we repent of our sins, then God will take us back as His children immediately. We are like His prodigal Son, who finally came home to his fathers' house.

John 14:1 *Let not your heart be troubled: you believe in God, believe also in me.*

John 14:11 *Believe Me that I am in the Father, and the Father in Me: or else believe Me for the very works' sake.* Faith is what we give God in return for all the good things He has done for us.

2. Next is the **Feast of Unleavened Bread**: A continuation process of strengthening our Faith. To achieve this, we have to remove our sin baggage by doing the following, though not stated in the verses **Lev. 23:6-14.** First, we have to humble ourselves by taking pride out of our life. Second, forgive those who have trespass against us and ask forgiveness for our trespass. The feast is 7 days to present our body, Holy and Perfect. In short a cleansing process. The eating of unleavened Bread points to the Body Christ, unblemished sacrificial Lamb of God.

In the New Testament; the eating of unleavened bread pertains to the breaking of the bread, the broken Body of Christ sacrificed at Calvary given up for us. Christ commands us to do the breaking of the bread ritual as often as we can to proclaim His death until He comes back.

3. After the 7 - day Feast of Unleavened Bread, the Sabbath, a Sunday, the Jews will observe the **Feast of First Fruits.** A feast offering: of the smaller of the first fruit harvest of the spring.

In the New Testament; this feast points to the Resurrection of Christ. We say: Christ is Risen. Christ is the First Fruit.

4. Then **the Day of the Pentecost** is celebrated 50 days after the day of Passover. The men shall offer the second small harvest unto the Lord. No man to come empty handed.

In the New Testament: The Holy Spirit came down from Heaven to perform Spiritual Baptism or Circumcision of the Heart on the believer or church. Thus opening a cut in the heart, thereby allowing the Holy Spirit to enter and dwell in the heart of the church/man. Making the believer, the temple of God. Immediately the church is grafted into the Vine, Read John 15:1, though the church/man is still alive in the flesh, he is now declared a **Member of the Body of Christ.**

At the first death of the member: the holy angels will carry the spirit to Paradise. As we picture verse **Luke 16:22** *And it came to pass, that the beggar died and was carried by the Angels into Abraham's bosom; the rich man also died and was buried.* God provides VIS treatment (very important spirit) if you are a Member of the Body of Christ, whereas the spirit of the unredeemed rich man went to Hell on his own to be tormented. Therefore if we go to hell we are on our own, there is nobody there to help us. Also riches if not properly used will not take us to Paradise but will lead us to Hell.

In Paradise: there will be no more problems, sickness, pain, sorrow and suffering, while waiting for the Second Coming of Christ. We will also be reunited with our loved ones who went before us we will see our brothers and sisters who are also redeemed. That is why Christ wants us to love our enemies in the natural world. Because if our enemies are also there, we cannot hate them, for there is no room for hate in Paradise.

As often as we can: we are to partake in the breaking of the bread and drinking the wine ritual to signify the eating of His Body and drinking His blood to proclaim His death.

5. **Feast of the Trumpets (Yom Kippur):** In the New Testament: We Christians, as followers of Christ, will stay in Paradise, while we wait for His Second Advent to be started by the blowing of the Trumpets. God will rupture His Church to meet Him in the clouds.

6. **Day of Atonement**: After the end of the battle of Armageddon, along with Christ we will bind Satan and send him to the bottomless pit so he can not deceive no more. Then we will gain our glorified bodies back. This I call: we are now certified Members of the Kingdom of God.

7. **Feast of the Tabernacles**: After receiving our glorified bodies back, we go to a booth to wait for the coming down of the New Jerusalem or New Heaven coming down.

8. The Last Great Day: There is no doubt: it will be the Greatest Day for the Church. A wedding feast is the event. The Bridegroom; Jesus Christ will wed His Bride, the Church. This is to certify the saints as bona fide citizens of the Kingdom of God. Christ ministry started in a wedding at Cana, Galilee and will culminate at His own wedding with the Church. The millennial Kingdom of God starts with Jesus Christ as the King. It is a Holy Day of celebration for Thy will be done on Earth as it is in Heaven. Amen.

We have to know and understand that in the present Church Age or Dispensation of Grace Period the will of our Father God on Earth is not total for will of man and of evil are still present on Earth.

Some Bible scholars say this day is the Great White Throne Judgment. I cannot agree because if this is a judgment day, it does not warrant our Lord to celebrate and have a feast. No one shall celebrate in judgment. It is similar to a maker or inventor who junked his work that did not pass quality control. It is a sad day for the Lord because His creations are judged to suffer.

These 8 Holy Days God marks a chronology of man's redemption process and intended solely for the Church or Believers. The Heavens celebrate if we accept Christ as Lord because we enter into a blood Covenant with Him. Unbelievers or the unredeemed are not part of these holy days celebration. If you are an unbeliever, ask yourself why?

In the New Testament, these Holy Days of God are mentioned but Christ did not command us to celebrate them. I believe they are all pointing to Him and each of the feast is Him. Now if we are in Christ, we have celebrated these Holy Days thru our all-in faith.

CHAPTER **15**

Jesus: I AM, The True Vine

The True Vine Explained: **John 15:1**, *I am the True Vine, and my Father is the Husbandman.* Father God is the Owner and Vinedresser of the Vineyard (Earth) and all that is in it; the True Vine (Jesus Christ) has its Jewish Roots in (Abraham, Isaac and Jacob the Patriarchs or forefathers by covenant); where all, the Fathers' blessings (to sustain) will flow to the branches (believers) and the fruits; See Fig. 1;

John 15:2 *Every branch in me that bears not fruit, He takes away: and every branch that bears fruit He purges it, that it bring forth more fruit.*

This explains what happens to those who had accepted Jesus Christ (church/believers) and who backslides (forgets or does not know where his blessings are coming from; and became unfaithful to Jesus Christ' commandments) and cannot overcome the temptation of this world, for they can not bear fruit then our Father cuts them off from being grafted into the Vine. Whereas, those who remained faithful to Him, He continuously groom, feed and clean for they obeyed and fulfilled the will of the Father.

Thus they will continue bearing fruit and more fruit. (God's gifts in abundance, i.e. love, kindness, patience, long suffering, courage, and children or fruit of the womb and etc.)

The most important of all is Love. If we learn how to use the gift of wisdom, it results in material gifts or mortal blessings.

John 15:3 *Now you are clean through the Word, which I have spoken unto you.* At this point the believer becomes holy or good, our sins are washed away, He sees us in the **Body of Christ,** everything (good) we ask for, will be granted.

John 15:4 *Abide in me, and I in you. As the branch cannot bear fruit of itself; except it abides in the Vine; no more can you, except you abide in Me.*

John 15:5 *I am the vine, you are the branches: he who abides in Me, and I in him, the same brings forth much fruit: for without Me you can do nothing.*

To illustrate verses 4 & 5 See Fig. 1: Imagine a vine, planted on the ground; you will see the earth, the roots, the vine, the branches and the leaves and the fruit. The branch's must objective or goal is to be permanently or forever connected or grafted into the vine.

The variables here are the branches, leaves and fruit. They can wither and be cut off anytime. What can the branch (believer or church or Israel of God or Christians or family (cell))? or High Priest do to prevent himself (why male, read 1 Cor. 11:3) from being cut off from the True Vine?

What can the branch or believer do; to stay connected to the Vine and keep the Blessings flowing?

- Never deny the Lordship of the Holy Spirit, for He is the Truth. The sin against the Holy Ghost is the only unforgivable sin mentioned in the Bible. Denial would mean unbelief and rebellion; with unbelief, we cannot submit or humble ourselves to God's will and commandments, and gives man no chance for salvation and atonement.

- Focus our faith and our eyes solely and continuously at the Finished Work of Jesus Christ at the Cross. The Object of Faith must be Jesus Christ and in Christ alone. No other object of faith can ever be a substitute.

- Never backslide, nor be lukewarm, neither boast or hate, don't commit spiritual adultery and don't envy others,

- Or do anything that will displease the Holy Spirit. Stay spiritually anchored by doing spiritual things; like obeying the first two Major Commandments of Jesus, basically stay in Love. If in everything we do, we do it in the context of Holy Love, bear fruit. I believe it will be very, very hard for Satan to tempt us. Even if he desires us, Christ will pray for us so that our Faith will not fail us.

Satan knows he was already defeated at Calvary.

John 15:6 *If a man abides not in Me, he is cast forth as a branch; and is withered; and men gathered them, and cast them into the fire, and they are burned.* Burned in the Lake of Fire.

John 15:7 *If you abide in Me, and my words abide in you shall ask what you will, and it shall be done unto you.* We will be blessed mightily.

Why do we have to bear good fruit? **John 15:8** *Herein is my Father Glorified, that you bear much fruit; so shall you be My Disciples.*

John 15:9 *As the Father has loved Me, so I have loved you: continue ye in my Love.* Be steadfast in Faith.

John 15:10 *If you keep My Commandments; you shall abide in My Love; even as I have kept My Father's Commandments, and I abide in His Love.* Christ showed us why it is so important to keep and abide in God's commandments for we rest in His love. Therefore our divine relationship with the Father keeps growing and bearing fruit. At the same we glorify God.

John 15:11 *These things have I spoken unto you, that My Joy might remain in you.*

John 15:12 *This is my Commandment, That you love one another, as I have loved you.* **All members of the Body of Christ** must love one another as brothers and sisters. We are one family, one body and one Kingdom. Hate cannot exist in this body.

John 15:13 *Greater love has no man than this, that a man lay down his life for his friends.* Nothing is greater than Christ dying on the cross for us to attain salvation. In the same way nothing is greater in this world than American military dying for freedom of people of other nation.

John 15:14 *You are my friends, if you do whatsoever I command you.* A true friend is loyal.

John 15:15 *Henceforth I call you not servants; for the servants knows not what the Lord does; but I called you friends; for all things that I have heard of my Father I have made known unto you.* This verse in the Bible that I like most: Calling us believers His friends instead of servants, revealing to us the ways of our Father. Now I am not ignorant of the economy of the Kingdom of God. Christ showed me the benefits of being a **Member of the Body of Christ.**

John 15:16 *You have not chosen Me, but I have chosen you, and ordained you; that you should go and bring forth fruit, and that your fruit should remain that whatsoever you shall ask of the Father in my Name, He may give it to you.* As members we are all Insiders, therefore anything we ask of from the Father it shall be given.

John 15:17 *These things I command you, that you love one another.* Verses 6 to 17 Generally states that as grafted member to the True Vine; that we are, an Insider in the Kingdom of God, more specifically the **Body of Christ.** This is more magnified by verse 16. That whatsoever, we ask from our Father in Heaven, He will give it to us in Jesus Name. What a wonderful promise, this no doubt, the Name above all Names.

Christ is the First Fruit of the Tree of Life:

Rom. 11:16 *For if the Firstfruit be Holy, the lump is also Holy and if the root be Holy, so are the branches.* Yes, if Christ is Holy being the First Fruit and so is the ground (lump, the Father), the root being

Abraham, Isaac and Jacob and the branches being the Church or believers in Christ are all HOLY. Now this is the family of Gods.

Rom. 11:17 *And if some of the branches be broken off, and you, being a wild olive tree were grafted among them, and will partake of the root and fatness of the olive tree.* Unlimited blessings.

Rom. 11:19 *Thou wilt say then, the branches were broken off, that I might be grafted in.* Gives us hope in being an adopted Son only through Faith in Christ.

Verses Rom11:16 to 19 farther illustrates John 15:4-5. In this case it is an olive tree. The lump being the earth or the Holy Father, the source of everything we are and what we need to live. The roots are our forefathers, Abraham, Isaac and Jacob, David and Solomon and Christ as Son of David being the First fruit and the Jews or Israel as the original branches, and the Gentiles being the grafted branches.

Because of unbelief (the Jews did not accept Christ as their Messiah in the first advent of Christ), the original branches, the Jews or Israel were broken off. And the Gentiles (the wild olive branch) did accept Christ as their Messiah and thus they were given the privilege to be grafted into the Olive Tree.

In these verses, the grafted Gentiles are advised not to boast against the original branches, the Jews, because time will come that the Jews will be grafted back to the Olive Tree. **And they will co-exist together in the Kingdom of God.** And hate has no place there. Any one who hates a brother cannot be a **Member of the Body of Christ.**

As of this writing, **I am urging my fellow Gentile Christians** to accept and love all our Jewish brothers now. We must extend our love, kindness and all the gifts we received from our Father in Heaven to our brothers in Israel. They need our support urgently. We must be a blessing to them. How can we say we love Jesus if we don't love the Jews as a brother? It is only, through loving them that we can let them know, God loves them. God uses our fellow man so we can feel God's love and intimacy. One of Christ's commands is: love one another as I have loved you.

Some Gentile Christian religious groups or sects, still despise the Jews, because in their doctrine, the Jews killed their Jesus, not understanding that the Jews had this Jesus first. They still don't know that every man and woman in this earth, are brothers and sisters in the Spirit, if we accept, Christ as our Lord and Saviour. This is why we pray that all may come to the Saving Grace of Christ, so we can grow the **Body of Christ.**

In this Church Age: the Israel of God are the Christian Gentiles and Christian Jews. There is no difference. They are the ones grafted to the Tree of Life, the True Vine, which is also Christ Jesus.

Who is Greater?

Matt. 23:17 *Ye fools and blind: for whether is greater, the gold or the temple that sanctifieth the gold?* As added validation, please read Matt. 23:19

A few things we must focus on:

1) Set your faith on the finished work of Christ on the cross as the means of our salvation.
2) Set your faith in love for Christ and fellowmen.
3) Set your faith in holiness of your spirit rather than material satisfaction.
4) Benchmark your holy spiritual position as to how your holy spiritual relationship with the Godhead by the measure of your faith. (Spiritual progress report)
5) Is the creation greater than the Creator? If the answer is not, why most of us oppose and disobey God's Commandments? Forget about temptation from Satan. In this moment of time, our generation is considered educated, we should not fall for this sin.

CHAPTER 16

Manasseh and Ephraim

The Now and the Future Symbolism for Jesus
Christ in the Church Age: Protectors of the Body
of Jesus Christ, Until He Comes Back.

The Blessing: **Gen 48:13** *And Joseph took them both, Ephraim on his right hand, towards Israel's left hand, and Manasseh in his left hand towards Israel right hand, and brought them near unto him.*

Gen. 48:14 *And Israel stretch out his right hand, and laid it upon Ephraim's head, who was the younger, and his left hand upon Manasseh's head, guiding his hands wittingly: for Manasseh was the first born*

Gen. 48:15 *And he blessed Joseph, and said, God, before whom my fathers Abraham and Isaac did walk, the God which fed me all my life long unto this day.*

Gen. 48:16 *And the Angel which redeemed me from all evil, bless the lads; and let my name be named on them, and the name of my* *fathers Abraham and Isaac, and let them grow into a multitude in the midst of the earth.*

Gen. 48:17 *And when Joseph saw that his father laid his right hand upon the head of Ephraim, it displeased him: and held up his fathers hand, to remove it from Ephraim's head unto Manasseh's head.*

Gen. 48:18 *And Joseph said unto his father; Not so, my father: for this the firstborn* (Manasseh); *put your right hand upon his head.*

Gen. 48:19 *And his father refused, and said, I know it my son, I know it: he also shall become a people, and he also shall be great: but truly his younger brother shall be greater than and his seed shall be a multitude of nations.*

Gen. 48:20 *And he blessed them that day, saying,* **in you shall Israel bless***, saying, God make you as Ephraim and as Manasseh: and he set Ephraim before Manasseh.* Please Continue reading Gen. 48:21-22, Joshua 24:32-33, 1 Chron. 5:2 and John 4:5: To have an idea what are these extra portion of land given to Joseph. **The double portion** went to Ephraim because he got the anointing of a birthright.

I believe that: In today's world; Ephraim is being symbolized by USA, and Manasseh is symbolized by UK. Why USA is Ephraim? 1) USA being a much bigger country than UK. 2) USA has more power (being a Superpower) than UK 3) USA was founded second and UK first. Obviously USA has received the double portion of Israel's blessings; and UK received single portion. These two countries are anointed: by the Most High God.

The above analysis was also validated in Tomorrow's World issue July-August, 2012 p15. It discussed that, "the birthrights promised to Isaac and Jacob were passed on to Manasseh and Ephraim".

Nevertheless; these two countries has wielded dominant power more than any other nation or nations on earth; or even combined: Plainly, very unprecedented. The blessings and presence of God is very evident, no matter where you look. There is justice in everything they do.

From the book Mystery of the Ages, by the late Herbert Armstrong, the founder and publisher of Plain Truth magazine and Ambassador College, he said USA is Manasseh and UK is Ephraim. Simply because; he believes USA is bowing down to UK. I say otherwise.

I believe that, God is using these two countries to control and police the whole world and to make them behave in order and to protect and grow His Church. As it is a continuous fulfillment of the prophecy: in Gen. 48:20 until now.

Gen. 22:17 *That in blessing I will bless you, and in multiplying I will multiply you, your seed are as the stars of the heaven, and as the sand which is upon the seashore; and your seed shall possess the gate of his enemies.*

Gen. 22:18 *And your seed shall the nations of the Earth be blessed, because you have obeyed My Voice.*

These two countries controlled all the shipping lanes (gates) from commercial maritime and military purposes for almost 300 years now.

Otherwise, Satan will always create every problem he can devise to destroy this Earth again. The same way he did when he ruled earth with his fellow fallen angels and the dinosaurs. He is already succeeding in promoting his theory of evolution by disguising it as science. Thus making the Dept of Education as his avenue to promote his deception. To further promote his opposition to God. The religious community has to find a way to counter his deception.

Furthermore, I believe there is another anointed country that is representative of; the **Body of Jesus Christ**. It is prophesied; in one of the books in the Bible by a minor prophet. This country is protected by UK and the USA. As if UK and USA is treating this little country as a little brother. This country is the Philippines.

In the Middle East: Why is Israel; surrounded by Islamic countries? I believe it is to fulfill Bible prophecies. Islamic religious leaders: wants to destroy and remove it from the map? They are so vocal of their evil intentions. You and I know that it is not going to happen, not this time. Only one of these countries recognizes Israel's right to exist as a nation. Why does Jordan is the only one among Israel's neighbors who truly accepts the Jewish nation's right to exist? Egypt's recognition of Israel is quasi. This only goes to validate how much Satan wants to defeat God even though he knows he was already defeated.

One obvious reason: Issau is Jordan and he is the older brother of Jacob. And Jacob is Israel. Even if Issau was cheated of his birthright, he let bygones be bygones. I guess blood is thicker than water as the saying goes.

In the Book of Revelation, the nation of Jordan will not be included in the Battle of Armageddon. It will be spared. Christ, the warrior will not smite Jordan. No biblical explanation.

CHAPTER 17

Jesus, I am The Truth

Furthermore, **John 14:15** *If you love Me, keep My Commandments*

John 14:16 *And I will pray the Father, and He shall give another Comforter, that He shall abide with you forever;*

John 14:17 *Even the Spirit of **Truth**; Whom the world cannot receive, because it sees Him not, neither knows Him; but you know Him; for He dwells with you. and shall be in you.*

John 14:18 *I will not leave you comfortless; I will come to you.* This proves that Jesus Christ, the Son, is also the Holy Spirit and the **TRUTH**.

John 14:26 *But the Comforter, which is the Holy Spirit, Whom the Father will send in My Name, He shall teach you all things, and bring all things to your remembrance, whatsoever I have said unto you.* Jesus foretold the coming of the Paraclete, the helper or advocate to help believers understand the **Truth** all about Him. We can say the Holy Spirit convicts our hearts of the Truth about Christ. This happened at the Feast of Pentecost. He also convicts our hearts if the temptation is so great that we are on the verge of committing sin. Therefore we cannot deny His work in us, if we do then we blaspheme the Holy Spirit and commit the unforgivable sin. We don't want to do this. So, brothers and sisters do not harden your hearts.

See also John 14:6 *I am The Way, **The Truth,** and The Life; no man comes unto the Father, but by Me.* In this verse, Jesus proclaims, who He really is. He leaves no more doubt about Him.

That in God's economy in Heaven is in Likeness of God's economy on earth.

Col 1:4 *Since we heard of **your Faith in Christ Jesus** and of the love which you have to all saints.* All the Members of the Body of Christ are saints, and in this one body all the members love on another as brothers and sisters. Hate has no place in this body.

Col. 1:5 *For the hope which is laid up for you in Heaven, whereof you heard before in **the Word of the Truth of the Gospel.***

Col. 1:6 *Which is come unto you, as it is in all the world; and brings forth fruit, as it does also in you, since the day you heard of it, and knew the **Grace of God in Truth.*** Faith, Hope and Love:

1 Tim 2:7 *Whereunto I am ordained a Preacher, and an Apostle, (I speak **the Truth** in Christ, and lie not) teacher of the Gentiles in faith and verity.* Teaching in Faith and in Trut*h*. Apostle Paul had to say these words to quench any doubt in him by the people he was teaching about Christ. Whenever we teach the Words of God anywhere, we will always experience dissent from our audience. So we must be patient. Allow the Holy Spirit to work on our behalf.

A report from a Missionary to Jordan, says that it takes 7.6 times on the average for a listener of the word of God to finally, find the strength to accept Christ Jesus as their Lord and Saviour. Therefore praying incessantly is required.

1 Tim 2:8 *I will therefore that men pray everywhere, lifting up holy hands, without wrath and doubting.*

Paul is saying here, that instead of complaining about people's unbelief that it would be better to pray that all men pray as well, lifting their holy hands up to the Lord so that they will be saved and does not hate and doubt his message which is from the Holy Spirit or the Truth. In praying we must call the unbeliever **by their names** so that our Father will also call them by their names, in the same manner as Jesus called the name of Lazarus. Please apply this method especially to our relatives and friends who are our loved ones.

When we witness and encounter people who does not want to accept Christ our Lord and Savior; it breaks our hearts because we know over a million times we are telling the Truth, we don't want these people to remain dead in the spirit. Our only option is to pray for those who are still lost.

The idea of a family structure setting exist in both dimension; spiritual and carnal. Father and Son. With this knowledge, how can we not love God? Just imagine, if you are father/husband who loves your family (works as a cell) and as most fathers does. You would love them no matter what. You will give them whatever they ask for. Biological Father's hearts are broken if they cannot provide.

Our Father in Heaven does the same; He loves us no matter what we have done. This gives man no excuse not to heed the Words of God. I call this, the Divine Parallel. **John 3:16**

John 8:31 *Then said Jesus to those Jews which believed on Him, If you continue in my word, then you are my Disciples indeed;* If we are Christ disciples, we are **Members of the Body of Christ.**

John 8:32 *And you shall know the Truth, and the Truth shall make you free.* Christ Jesus is the Truth. And must be understood that Jesus is the Holy Spirit. Christ is not talking about literal truth. And it is Christ who always sets us free if we believe. **See John 14:6.**

So many people talks about the truth and that it shall set you free, and usually they mean the literal truth. Thus, it has no spiritual value.

John 8:34 *Jesus answered them, Verily, verily, I say unto you, Whosoever commits sin is the servant of sin.* This verse validates that sin has two components: one is the temptation of the Devil and the other is our acceptance of the temptation is equal to Sin. Once we sin against God, we are in bondage to Satan and become servant of him. And if we are of this world, we serve Satan.

To illustrate why we serve God: Take a good look at how almost all Christian nations behave these days. It is pretty much calm they don't go to war against each other and I believe we have learned to love and serve one another as commanded by Christ. If we can do this, surely the blessing will keep flowing. I thank and pray to God the Father, Christ and the Holy Spirit that this good situation will continue and improve until Christ comes. The last war between Christians has ended about 2 decades ago in Northern Ireland. It shows that Christians have come a long way Baby, that we are united as one in the **Body of Christ.**

And who are serving Evil? Look at what is happening to most non-Christian nations? I don't need to elaborate. You make your own judgment.

If there is a war in a Christian nation, it is usually between a non-Christian ideology and the ruling Christian government.

Healing

Members of the Body of Christ can ask our Father to heal us of our sickness by praying that we be healed. Try it. He responds immediately. That is my testimony.

CHAPTER 18

Preparation: Second Advent

Jesus Christ, I am The Bread of Life
At His Last Supper: Three versions of 3 Gospel.

Matthew 26:26 *And as they were eating, Jesus took the bread, and blessed it, and broke it, and gave it to the Disciples, and said, Take, eat; this is My Body.*

Mark 14:22 *And as did eat; Jesus took bread, and blessed, and broke it, and gave them; and said: Take; eat: this is my Body.*

Luke 22:14 *And when the hour was come, He sat down, and the 12 apostles with Him,*

Luke 22:15 *And He said unto them. With desire I have desired to eat this Passover with you before I suffer.*

Luke 22:16 *For I say unto you, I will not anymore eat thereof; until it be fulfilled in the Kingdom of God.*

Luke 22:17 *And He took the cup, and gave thanks, and said, Take this, and divide it among yourselves.*

Luke 22:18 *For I say unto you, I will not drink of the fruit of the vine, until the Kingdom of God shall come.* Christ second coming.

Luke 22:19 *And He took bread, and gave thanks, and broke it, and gave unto them, saying: This is my Body, which is given for you: do this in remembrance of me.*

Luke 22:20 *Likewise also the cup after supper, saying; **This cup is the New Testament in My Blood, which is shed for you.***

The broken bread that He gave the Disciples at His Last Supper represents the broken Body of Jesus Christ at His Crucifixion. It fulfills the outpouring of the Holy Spirit (being the Spiritual body cell of Christ) at the Feast of Pentecost (50 days after the Crucifixion). Now the Holy Spirit is available to all who believes. This allows the Holy Spirit to dwell individually in the hearts of those who have accepted Jesus Christ as their Lord and Savior and Him Crucified. At Pentecost all who have accepted Christ's shedding of His Blood for the remission of Sins started speaking in tongues. And they understood each other, because they are now one in Christ by virtue of the baptism of the Holy Spirit. The Power of the New Testament is now in effect. Those who believed are now grafted into the **True Vine, Jesus Christ.**

1 Cor. 11:23 Apostle Paul speaking: *For I have received of the Lord that which I also delivered unto you, That the Lord Jesus the same night in which He was betrayed took bread:*

1 Cor. 11:24 *And when He had given thanks, He brake it, and said, Take, eat: this is my body, which is broken for you: do this in remembrance of Me.*

The eating of the bread as Body of Jesus allows the believer's spirit to be part **or Member of the Body of Christ** in preparation for His second advent.

1 Cor. 11:25 *After the same manner also he took the cup, when He had supped, saying, This cup is the New Testament in my blood, this do ye, as oft as you drink it, in remembrance of Me.* Jesus urges His Church to do this ritual as often as we can to maintain and I believe assure the Church of its continuous relationship with Him.

1 Cor. 11:26 *For as often as you eat the bread, and drink this cup, you do show the Lord's death till He come.* This is to proclaim His and our victory over Satan and to encourage all who witness this gesture or ritual to also believe.

1 Cor. 11:27 *Wherefore whosoever shall eat of this bread, and drink this cup of the Lord, unworthily, shall be guilty of the Body and Blood of the Lord.* Any one who is not spiritually prepared to eating of the bread and drinking of the wine especially earmarked for this ritual will be subject to Judgment, and is similar to using the name of the Lord in vain.

1 Cor. 11:28 *But let the man examine himself, and so let him eat of that bread, and drink of that cup.* Allow the unbeliever to check his heart if he truly believes and is not playing games or pretending to be one of them just to please someone.

Jesus, the Living Bread

John 6:51 *I am the Living Bread which came down from Heaven: if any man eat of this bread, he shall live forever and the bread which I will give is my flesh, which I will give for the life of the world.* His body will come back as the Holy Spirit and will sanctify all human spirit who will accept Him as Lord, to grow the **Body of Christ.**

1 Cor. 11:29 *For he who eats and drinks unworthily, eats and drinks damnation to himself, not discerning the Lord's Body.* Pertains to one who has not accepted Christ as Lord and Savior, and has not committed his spirit to the Father for lack of understanding. We must be born of God first.

1 Cor. 11:30 *For this cause many are weak and sickly among you, and many sleep.*

He, who has used the things of God in vain cannot be a **Member of the Body Christ**, therefore he cannot receive the blessings or provision flowing from the Father through Jesus and unto the believer or branch.

It is useless anyway to partake of the bread and wine, if that person is not committed to believing Christ. God's blessings cannot flow to him, for he does not have a relationship with the Father through Christ.

CHAPTER 19

Seven (7) Churches

These seven Churches must be understood even partially correct. There are many attempts of interpretations and I will not say that the others are wrong. I pray that my explanation will be enough for the reader to assimilate some of its meaning and importance: in order to have a working understanding on why it is important to know how to be a **Member of the Body of Christ.**

The 7 Churches are 7 different types of believers and it still applies to all churches until the dispensation of God's grace has run its course, or when the gathering of the **Body of Christ** is completed. In the course of our Christian life in the flesh or even though we already accepted Christ as Lord and Savior, some of us still retain some Pagan traditions, beliefs of the old, or rituals influenced by our past religious beliefs that we feel and think are good and worthy. We ran off course in our attempt to finish the race in faith. Some of these stumbling blocks are put in place: by Satan. Who is your and God's enemy. God does not want us to carry the old baggage anymore. We have to focus our faith unto Jesus and only Jesus and Him Crucified. Knowing and rejecting evil is a positive step in keeping our focus at the prize. We are told to remember where we have fallen and repent and find our way back to the love of Christ.

Remember these stumbling blocks, prevents the believer to be a permanent **Member of the Body of Christ.**

Church of Ephesus

Rev. 2:1 *Unto the Angel of the Church of Ephesus write: These things says He who holds the seven stars in His Right Hand, Who walks in the midst of the Seven Golden Candlesticks:*

Rev.2: 2 *I know your works, and your labour, and your patience, and how you, cannot bear them which are evil; and you have tried them which say they are Apostles, and are not, and have found them liars:*

Rev. 2:3 *And have borne, and have patience, and for My Name's sake have labored, and have not fainted.*

Rev. 2:4 *Nevertheless I have somewhat against you cause you have left your first love.*

Rev. 2:5 *Remember therefore from where you are fallen, and repent, and do the first works; or else I will come unto you quickly, and remove your candlestick out of his place, except you repent.*

Rev. 2:6 *But this you have, that you hate the deeds of the Nicolaitanes, which I also hate.*

Rev. 2:7 *He who has an ear, let him hear what the Spirit says unto the Churches; To him who overcomes will I give to eat of the tree of life, which is in the midst of the Paradise of God.* Bread of Life.

The Church of Ephesus is a type of church (believer). I believe that this church was really very overzealous in its proselytizing efforts. They deviated from the doctrine of Love. But believed in Jesus Christ as their Lord and Saviour and Him Crucified.

This church cannot love the unlovely, instead of sharing the Love we receive from our Lord Jesus, this believer resorted to using hatred measures to rebuke or perhaps use some of manipulative measures to convert the wicked.

They forgot that if we love one another, we actually show and let the brothers and sisters feel that the Lord Jesus Loves them: Especially to unbelievers. And if this unsaved person feels God's Love, we know and we pray that they will be changed and be just like us who are **Members of the Body of Christ,** a 100 fold Christian.

Our Goal as a Church: **To be a full time, permanent and sanctified Member of the Body of Christ.**

Church of Smyrna

Rev. 2:8 *And unto the Angel of the Church in Smyrna write; These things says the First and the Last, which was dead and is alive.*

Rev. 2:9 *I know your works, and tribulation, and poverty (but you are rich) and I know the blasphemy of them; which say they are Jews, and are not, but are synagogue of Satan.*

Rev. 2:10 *Fear none of those things; which you shall suffer: Behold the Devil shall cast some of you into prison, that you may be tried and you shall have tribulation ten days: be thou faithful unto death, and I will give you a Crown of Life.*

Rev. 2:11 *He who has an ear, let him hear what the Spirit says unto the Churches; He who overcomes shall not be hurt of the second death.*

The Church of Smyrna are the persecuted churches or believers in Christ Jesus, around the world. Persecuted for their Faith in Christ.

Many communist countries like North Korea, and China are persecuting Christians. The worst are Islamic countries like Saudi Arabia, Iran, Somalia, Iraq and Syria to name a few. These countries, also called Principalities of Evil. They have a very high violation of Human Individual Rights for persecuting Christians and Jews and killing them for their Faith. Islam is the most anti-Christian and anti-Jewish religion in the world.

It is a crime to carry a Holy Bible when traveling in these countries. It is punishable by death. The Koran instructs its followers that it is holy to commit these crimes.

In my view, Islam is Satanic. It is copycat of Judaism. They distorted it and it became a counterfeit religion. Islam preaches a doctrine of hate. Still I consider them as my potential brothers and sisters. They are just deceived big time. Christ can transform them all.

Therefore, Christians in this countries mentioned above must hold fast to their Faith and remain faithful unto death. It's like an advanced Great Tribulation period for over 100 million Christians living in these countries, and we must pray for their soul and spirit that they suffer not.

Church of Pergamos

Rev. 2:12 *And to the Angel of the Church in Pergamos write: These things said He which had the sharp sword with two edges;*

Rev. 2:13 *I know your works, and where you dwell, even where Satan's seat is: and you hold fast My Name, and have not denied My Faith, even in those days wherein Antipas was My Faithful martyr, who was slain among you, where Satan dwells.*

Rev. 2:14 *But I have a few things against you, because you have there them who hold the doctrine of Balaam, who taught Balac to cast a stumbling block before the Children of Israel, to eat things sacrificed unto idols, and to commit fornication.*

Rev. 2:15 *So have you also them who hold the doctrine of the Nicolaitanes, which thing I hate.*

Rev. 2:16 *Repent or else I will unto you quickly, and will fight against them with the sword of my mouth.*

Rev. 2:17 *He who has an ear, let him what the Spirit says unto the Churches; To him that overcomes will I give to eat of the hidden Manna, and will give him a white stone, and in the stone a new name written, which no man knows saving he who receives it.*

The Church of Pergamos: These type of Churches are the Jewish Christians living all around the world who have received and heard the Gospel of Christ. They were the scattered Jews and have hang on to their culture and religious rituals. Although they profess to be True Christians, they still hold on to false doctrine of another gods, including believing and practicing black magic and eating foods sacrificed to idols.

In essence this church is committing spiritual adultery. And much worse the unholy practices becomes a stumbling block for the Children of Israel, to accept Jesus Christ as their Messiah and Savior, and become **Members of the Body of Christ.**

Also, this church listens and believes in doctrines (Nicolaitanees) that are not Biblical in context, more of myth and superstitions instead on putting their faith exclusively on the Cross of Christ.

Church of Thyatira

Rev. 2:18 *And unto the Angel of the Church in Thyatira write: These things saith the Son of God, Who has His eyes like unto a flame of fire, and his feet are like fine brass;*

Rev. 2:19 *I know your works, and charity, and service, and faith, and your patience; and you works; and the last to be more that the first.*

Rev. 2:20 *Notwithstanding I have a few things against you, because you suffer that woman Jezebel, which call herself a Prophetess, to teach and to seduce My servants to commit fornication, and to eat things Sacrificed unto idols.*

Rev. 2:21 *And I gave her space to repent of her fornication, and she repented not.*

Rev. 2:22 *Behold; I will cast her into a bed and them who commit adultery with her into great tribulation, except they repent of their deeds.*

Rev. 2:23 *And I will kill her children with deaths; and all the Churches shall know that I am He who searches the reins and hearts; and I will give unto every one of you according to your works.*

Rev. 2:24 *But unto you I say, and unto the rest in Thyatira, as many as have not this doctrine, and which have not known the depths of Satan, as they speak; I will put upon you none other burden.*

Rev. 2:25 *But that you have already hold fast till I come.*

Rev. 2:26 *And he who overcomes, and keeps My works unto the end, to him will I give power over the nations.*

Rev. 2:27 *And he shall rule them with a rod of iron, as the vessels of a potter shall they be broken to shivers, even as I received of My Father.*

Rev. 2:28 *And I will give him the Morning Star*

Rev. 2:29 *And who has an ear, let him hear what the Spirit says unto the Churches.*

The Church of Thyatira can be interpreted as: The type of church: those who believes in Salvation by works primarily. I believe, it is because the brother of Jesus, James, who wrote the Book of James that says: "A faith without works is a dead faith" I see nothing wrong with this verse. I believe the Romans being very work oriented, so they adopted Doctrine of Salvation by works, and by Faith second. Forgetting that Faith comes by hearing the every Word that proceeds from the mouth of God. And works is a product and validation of Faith. Why work on something you do not believe in.

Believers are trying very, very hard to please God with working hard, sacrificing their body unto exhaustion. This not what God want. God desires Worship rather than sacrifice. Worship is meat for our God. I believe in the same manner rebellion against God is meat for Satan, therefore do not oppose God as it makes the accuser stronger and our lives more miserable. Why? Gods blessings and protection stops flowing to us.

Church of Sardis

Rev. 3:1-6 *And unto the Angel of the Church of Sardis write: These things saith He Who has the Seven Spirits of God, and the Seven Stars; I know your works, that you have a name that you live; and are dead.*

Rev 3:2 *Be watchful, and strengthen the things; which remain, that are ready to die: for I have not found your works perfect for God.*

Rev. 3:3 *Remember therefore how you have received and heard, and hold fast, and repent. If therefore you shall not watch, I will come on you as thief, and you shall not know what hour I will come upon you.*

Rev. 3:4 *You have a few names even in Sardis, which have not defiled their garments; and they shall walk with Me in white: for they are worthy.*

Rev. 3:5 *He who overcomes, the same shall be clothe in white raiment; and I will not blot out his name out of the Book of Life, but I will confess his name before My Father, and before His Angels.*

Rev. 3:6 *He who has an ear, let him hear what the Spirit says unto the Churches.*

The Church of Sardis is a type of believers who have heard and received the Gospel of Jesus Christ. They have proven that they are seasoned Christians for some time and have manifested that they love the Lord Jesus.

But these are believers that after receiving and hearing the Gospel of Christ, took their faith for granted and continued to pursue other cares for the carnal ways, rather than being consistently watchful of the spiritual ways of God. They are the backsliders and failed to develop a real spiritual relationship with our Father through Lord Jesus. Furthermore they failed to validate their faith by not working on the will of the Father and finishing it. Obviously they were cut-off from the True Vine or are on the verge of being cut-off.

They think they are already saved after hearing and receiving the Gospel of Christ and confident their names are listed in the Book of Life; that they have eternal life, but in reality they did backslide and took their faith for granted and still remain spiritually dead.

Now they must find their way back to their first Love, Jesus Christ.

Church of Philadelphia

Rev. 3:7 *And unto the Angel of the Church of Philadelphia write: These things says He Who is Holy, He who is true, He who has the key of David, He Who opens, and no man shuts; and shuts, and no man opens.*

Rev. 3: 8 *I know your works: behold I have set before you an open door, and no man can shut it: for you have little strength, and kept my Word, and have not denied My Name.*

Rev. 3:9 *Behold, I will make them of the Synagogue of Satan, which says they are Jews, and are not, but do lie; behold I will make them to come and worship before your feet, and to know that I have loved you.*

Rev. 3:10 *Because you have kept My Word of My patience, I also will keep you from the hour of temptation, which shall come upon all the world, to try them who dwell upon the earth.*

Rev. 3:11 *Behold, I come quickly: hold that fast which you have, that no man take your crown.*

Rev. 3:12 *Him who overcomes will I make a pillar in the Temple of My God, and he shall go no more out; and I will write upon him the name of My God, and the name of the City of My God, which is New Jerusalem, which comes down out of Heaven from my God and I will write upon him My new Name.*

Rev. 3:13 *He who has an ear, let him hear what the Spirit says unto the Churches.*

The Church of Philadelphia is the type of Believer that glorifies the Lord Jesus Christ.

The type of believer we should be all like. A church that is; grafted to the True Vine, and bears more fruit. All he has to do is make sure that his faith, fail him not.

Verse 10 Amplifies the total protection from any temptation of evil provided by Jesus. WOW.

He is the type of church that he is in this world but not of this world. These are the Members of the Body of Christ.

This church is a sanctified member of the Body of Christ. All he has to do is "hold that fast which you have" Don't ever think of backsliding.

A 100 fold Christian. Who can love the unlovely and expect nothing in return. Are we this type of church? I pray that all believers will be this type.

Church of Laodecea

Rev. 3:14 *And unto the Angel of the Church of the Laodeceans write: These things says the Amen, the faithful, and true witness, the beginning of the Creation of God.*

Rev. 3: 15 *I know your works; that you are neither cold nor hot: I would you were cold or hot.*

Rev. 3:16 *So then because you are lukewarm, and neither cold nor hot; I will spue you out of My mouth.*

Rev. 3:17 *Because you say I am rich, and increased with goods, and have need of nothing; and knowest not that you are wretched, and miserable, and poor, and blind, and naked:*

Rev. 3:18 *I counsel you to buy of Me gold tried in the fire, that you may be rich; and white raiment, that you may be clothed, and that the shame of your nakedness do not appear; and anoint your eyes with eyesalve, that you may see.*

Rev. 3:19 *As many as I love, I rebuke and chasten: be jealous therefore, and repent.*

Rev. 3:20 *Behold I stand at the door, and knock: if any man hear My voice, and open the door, I will come into him, and will sup with him, and be with Me.*

Rev. 3:21 *To him who overcomes will I grant to sit with Me in My Throne.*

Rev. 3:22 *He who has an ear, let him hear what the Spirit says unto the Churches.*

The Church of Laodecea is a type of believer that is faithful, accepts the fact that there is a Creator, he reads the Holy Bible from Genesis to Revelation and obviously goes to church or mass regularly. He is a member of a congregation and is all Amen to whatever the Pastor says.

Most likely; this church is not sincere in his worship, just to get through the motion. They are content just to be seen in Church. They are not spiritually motivated to serve the Lord. Lukewarm worship is not pleasing to God. It does not bear Fruit.

Verse 17 implies that the Laodecean church (believer) is not a cheerful giver. In short he is a miser, a reluctant giver and probably only gives pennies and change, a believer with no expression of spiritual gratitude to the Lord Jesus Christ. He does not understand the value and importance of giving.

When God ask for tithes and offering, churches like Laodecea thinks that it is an obligation rather than a privilege. They don't know that it is better to give than receive.

In verse 18, Jesus challenges us to give more than Mal. 3:10 stipulates, and be expectant of abundant blessings in return. God wants us to be an Eph 3:20 believer. Or to say giving more to the Lord to show that he loves Jesus Christ. Because Jesus did loved us first. It is just fitting that we give back love to our Lord. Be a servant to one another.

Eph 3:19 *And to know the Love of Christ, which passes knowledge, that you might be filled with all the fullness of God.*

Eph. 3:20 *Now unto Him who is able to do exceeding abundance above all that we ask or think according to the powers that works in us.*

Verse 20-22, Jesus promised us the rewards, if we repent and do His will, the things that glorify God. Giving to the Lord more than tithes and Love Offering.

Example: King Solomon offered over a thousand Offerings to show that he loves God, and when ask by the Lord what he wants, he chose to have wisdom rather than material wealth, and the Lord gave him everything anyway. We can just imagine how plenty was his material blessings from the Lord. **King Solomon was hot for the Lord.** Someone we can emulate how to love the Lord.

Verse 19. I, for one believed at first that it was the act of King Solomon asking for wisdom rather than material things that prompted God to give him every thing, or abundant blessings. But now I know better.

He was hot for God first and foremost. Actually, the Lord wants us to be jealous of those He has lavishly blessed, so we copy and emulate those who love the Lord Christ unconditionally.

Summary: Check out for yourself; (my motto: if you are in doubt, be sure to check it out) **If the measure of your Faith** criteria falls in any of the 7 churches except Philadelphia, then you need to really, really examine, where you stumbled, get up and check what is your position as far as relationship with Jesus, our Savior is concerned. Remember the 30, 60, and 100 fold. **(Deut. 16:16, Mark 4:20, Matt. 13:8)**

As far as I am concerned, I would aim for the 100 fold, which means unlimited Faith equals unlimited love also equals unlimited blessings.

Unlimited blessing means, we are blessed financially, romantically, physically and spiritually. I mean everything or in all aspect of our life. At the same time you can also love the unlovely. All the blessings we receive must also be given freely. And our Father will give us more. We can only do this, if we are, **a Member of the Body of Christ.**

We have been warned to go back where we stumble, and then get up from it, overcome and move on to the right path to becoming a permanent resident **Member in the Body of Christ.** I believe this is the main purpose of learning about the different types of Churches of the Church Age.

As believers, we know how we measure up. Are we justified by faith to be grafted in the True Vine? And be guaranteed to receive the blessings and privileges promised by God the Father?

CHAPTER **20**

Who is Santo Nino?

Now that we have discussed: Who is Jesus Christ and Who are the Churches, and we now have a fairly clear understanding of these topics in the Holy Bible; then we can tackle the most Important Topic of this Book. To unlock: Who is the **Body of Christ.** Please fasten your seatbelts. Keep reading.

The History of Santo Nino de Cebu, Holy Child of Prague, Santo Nino de Atocha and Statue of Mechlin.

First, let us look into a history background of Santo Nino de Cebu at Wikipidea.com and other sites of the Internet: Excerpts and I quote:

Santo Nino de Cebu (Holy Child of Cebu) is a celebrated Roman Catholic vested statue of the Child Jesus venerated by many Catholic Filipinos who believe it to be miraculous.

The image of Santo Nino, measures approximately 12 inches tall, the statue is believe to be originally made in Flanders, Belgium, and is highly similar in iconography to the Infant Jesus of Prague. The statue is clothed in its distinctive and expensive red manto, and bears regalia that include a gold crown, globus cruciger, and scepter mostly donated from devotees in the Philippines and abroad.

It is permanently housed in a bullet- proofed glass at the Basilica Minore del Santo Nino in Cebu City.

Its feast is celebrated every third Sunday of January.

HISTORY:

On September 29, 1519, a fleet of 5 Galleons commanded by Portuguese Navigator Ferdinand Magellan at the service of the King and Queen of Spain set sail from San Lucas de Barrameda to search for the Spice Islands and some historians says: to find a westward route to the Indies. They did not find exactly the spice island but instead landed in Limasawa, a small island south of Leyte in the central part of the Philippines. Magellan took possession of the islands and named it after King Philip of Spain.

In April 1521, Ferdinand Magellan, arrived in Cebu. He persuaded Raja Humabon and his chief wife Humaway, to pledge their allegiance to Spain. They were later baptized into the Catholic faith, taking the Christian names Carlos (after the Holy Roman Emperor Carlos V) and Juana (after Joanna of Castille, his mother).

According to Antonio Pigafetta, an Italian chronicler to the Spanish expedition, Ferdinand Magellan handed Pigafetta the image to be given to the Raja's wife right after the baptismal rites officiated by Padre Pedro Valderama.

As it was Pigafetta himself who personally presented the Santo Nino to the newly baptized Queen Juana as a symbol of alliance, her newly baptized husband King Carlos, Magellan presented the bust of "Ecce Homo", or the depiction of Christ before Pontious Pilate. He then presented the Virgin Mary to the natives who were baptized after their rulers.

Magellan died on April 27, 1521 in the Battle of Mactan, at the hands of Mactan's chieftain Lapu-Lapu, leaving the image behind. Legends say that after initial efforts by the natives to destroy it, the image was venerated as the animist creation Bathala.

On April 28, 1565, Spanish mariner Juan de Camus finds the statue in a pine box amidst the ruins of a burnt house. The image carved from wood and coated with paint, stood 30 cm tall, and wore a loose velvet garment, a gilded neck chain, and a woolen red hood. A golden sphere, a replica of the world, was in the left hand, and the right hand is slightly raised in benediction.

Camus presented the image to Miguel Lopez de Legazpi and the Agustinian Priest; the natives refused to associate it with the gift of Magellan, claiming it had existed it there since ancient times. Writer Dr. Resil Mojares wrote that the natives did so for fear that the Spaniards would demand it back.

The natives' version of the origin of the Santo Nino was in the Agipo (Stump or Driftwood) legend, which states that, the statue was caught by a fisherman, who chose to get rid of it, only to have it returned with a plentiful harvest.

The statue was later taken out for procession; afterwards which Legazpi then ordered the creation of Confraternity of the Santo Nino de Cebu, appointing Father Andres de Urdaneta as head Superior. Legazpi instituted a fiesta to commemorate the finding of the image, and the original celebration still survives today.

The Minor Basilica of Santo Nino de Cebu (Spanish: Basilica Menor del Santo Nino de Cebu), was built on the spot where the image was found by Juan de Camus. The parish was originally made out of bamboo and mangrove and claims to be the oldest parish in the Philippines. Pope Paul IV elevated its rank as Minor Basilica on its 400th year Anniversary.

Comments: What was really the purpose of the westward voyage by Ferdinand Magellan to the Indies other than to look for the Spice Islands?

First of all, they carried 3 Catholic images: the statue of Holy Child Jesus, the Ecce-Homo, and the Virgin Mary. I believe Father God spoke to the Spanish Royal Family that they have to proselytize along the way. And these 3 images are to be given away as a symbol of accepting the Catholic Faith.

I also believe there is a spiritual reason why the natives invented or made up the story that the image was not brought by the Spaniards but was an original of the islands. The image of Santo Nino de Cebu wants to stay in the Philippine Islands because it is prophesied in one of the Old Testament Books. The Philippines is His headquarters. We will find out as we move on.

Santo Nino de Cebu,
The Image of Holy Child Jesus

For Images of the Santo Nino de Cebu, please check the Wikipidea.com/ Santo Nino page and other sites.

The Miracles

1) Forty–four years later, in 1565, Cebu for a big part was destroyed by fire. The fire was set on purpose by the Spaniards as a punishment for hostile activities by the Cebuanos. In one of the burned houses, a Spanish soldier found the image of Santo Nino, remarkably unscathed! Since then the miraculous image has been treated as a patron Saint by the Cebuanos.

2) During the last World War, a bomb fell inside the Church but the image was recovered unscathed. This is one of the numerous miracles and powers attributed to the Holy Image; to list a few. There are more account of miracles, please check out www.sacs-stvi.org

There are a few Internet sites, alongside with that gives reverence and veneration to Santo Nino. That says; in doing so could be equivalent to idolatry. There are many claims and accusations that the Roman Catholics are guilty of idolatry. The warning is appreciated. Thank you.

Let us discuss what the Holy Bible say about idolatry.

Lev 26:1 *You shall make you no idols nor graven image, neither rear you up a standing image, neither shall you set up any image of stone in your land, to bow down unto it: for I am the Lord your God.*

Deut. 5:8 *You shall not make you any graven image, or any likeness of any thing that is in heaven above, or that is in the Earth beneath, or that is in the waters beneath the Earth:*

Deut. 5:9 *You shall not bow yourself unto them: for I the Lord your God am a jealous God, visiting the iniquity of the fathers upon the children unto the third and fourth generation of them who hate Me.*

Verse 8. **"Graven image" are images of those things that are dead, meaning has no living spirit or no spirit at all**: example: animals, plants, stones, fallen angels or other inanimate objects. In "heaven above" no humans have been or seen what is heaven like; so man cannot paint a tangible picture of something he has not seen in Old Testament time,

"Earth beneath" is the dwelling place for the fallen angels by daylight and "waters beneath" are dwelling place for the fish and are not a habitat for man. Man cannot live or dwell in these two environments, and so the creations in these conditions are all dead, "similarly graven images". Even images of holy angels: for they were not created in the image of God. And besides holy angels are 1 rank lower than the sanctified spirit of man.

Therefore, making the image of man or making the image of Jesus Christ or the saints is not restricted or prohibited and reverence does not constitute idolatry. Man is made in the image of God and Likeness, and has a living Spirit. It is important that we must know the image of our Father in Heaven even through statues, for it is the way to put a name into a face. God has a form though He is a Spirit. We now know what is His form and His form is that of a man. The Scriptures tells us to worship the great I AM in spirit (image) and in truth. We cannot worship the wood or stone that makes the image. Jesus told His disciples: if you have seen Me you have seen the Father. The Scriptures says the saints are God-like in images.

Well perhaps there is an exception: we cannot venerate the image of Hitler, I cannot say for sure with Hitler (although archives say he committed suicide by gunshot, but no witnesses) but most likely, he has a graven image, because he orchestrated the murder of over 6 million Jews in World War II, the Lord said vengeance is mine and for sure Hitler has to repay, and I believe his spirit is dead.

Thus, making and venerating image Jesus Christ must not be restricted and must not be construed as idolatry. Verse 9: "Do not bow". Worshipping these graven images and likeness; is forbidden by Our Lord. It is tantamount to spiritual adultery.

"Visiting the iniquity" applies only to those parents that did not accept Jesus Christ as their Lord and Savior. But the children becoming a born-again in the spirit of Christ, breaks the curse.

The course of worship must be in spirit and in truth. And if we pray in spirit and in truth, we know that Our True God listens and answers prayers. Try it. Get yourself ready to listen to His little small voice.

Col. 2:8 *Beware lest any man spoil you through philosophy and vain deceit, after the tradition of men, after the rudiments of the world, and not after Christ.* Go watch and pray everyday. For our enemies are many. Let no vain deceit fool you, with God's Word, we are smarter than the devil.

Col 2:9 *For in Him* (Christ) *dwells all the fullness of the Godhead bodily.*

Verse 8: Pertains to anyone preaching away from the doctrine of Redemption from Sin through Jesus Christ. If anyone does it, we must not listen. We must make sure their doctrine of faith is after Christ' work at the Cross: as the means. It is this Work that paid our sin debt. A cross without Christ in it does not mean anything for it is only an object.

A cross without Christ hanging in it is not holy, for only Christ is Holy. Christ makes everything Holy. That is why if **Christ is in us and us in Christ, we are Holy.**

Verse 9 The "Godhead bodily" is Christ. He is the completion and the fullness of Deity and in Him the believer is also complete.

CHAPTER 21

The Body of Christ

In a Revelation I got from the Holy Spirit, the Holy Child Jesus, the Santo Nino de Cebu, the Body of Christ and the Christ of the Second Advent are one and the same.

In the revelation, the Santo Nino is about the size of a 6 years old boy, about more than 3 feet high at this time; February 14, 2014. The question is: Why is Jesus Christ a **small Boy again?** When in fact He was a full grown Man, when He was crucified and then ascended unto Heaven, after spending 40 days with His Disciples on Earth after His Resurrection? Now we will uncover these mysteries.

What or Who is the Body of Jesus Christ in His First Advent:

Luke 1:30 *And the angel said unto her, Fear not, Mary: for thou hast found favour with God.*

Luke 1:31 *And behold, thou shalt conceived in thy womb, and bring forth a Son, and shalt call His name Jesus.*

Luke 1:32 *He shall be great and shall be called, the Son of the Highest: and the Lord God shall give unto Him the throne of His father David.*

Luke 1:35 *And the Angel answered and said unto her, the Holy Spirit shall come upon you, and the power of the Highest shall overshadow you: therefore also that the holy thing which shall be born of you shall be called the Son of God.*

These verses explained: **What constitute the Body of Jesus Christ in His First Coming?** The boy named Jesus is made up of the Spirit of God and the flesh and blood of a woman named Mary. The "holy thing" born is without Sin. Joseph and Mary raised the boy up.

When Christ was 30 years old He started His Ministry by transforming the water into the best wine ever, at a wedding in Cana, Galilee, which was attended by His mother Mary and some of His Disciples.

At the Last Supper of Christ before Passover: He broke the bread and said to His Disciples this is My Body, and eat of it, which will be given up for you. Every cell of Christ' Body, which He gave up for man's sin at His Crucifixion came back at the Feast of Pentecost as the Holy Spirit. Thus Christ's promise that the Father will send His disciples the Comforter, Counselor or the Paraclete was fulfilled.

After His Last Supper: Jesus Christ has to die at the Cross and to redeem man from his bondage to Satan. Jesus Blood was shed in 7 different parts of His Body to complete the purchase arrangement and after that Satan has no more power over man if man will reject Satan. And man is now ready, and willing to come back to his original owner, Father God.

Ladies and Gentlemen: To weaken Evil in this world: ALL of us must reject Satan's guile and deception, for he is the thief, the killer, the destroyer and the liar. We must have Faith in Christ only, that He has redeemed us and paid our debts on the cross at Calvary and now we have a way to come back to Paradise, where Adam and Eve had lived before the fall. Paradise is our home: we can go to the Garden east of Eden because we find favor with God.

At Feast of Pentecost: Exactly 50 days after Christ was crucified.

Acts 2:1 *And when the Day of Pentecost was fully come, they were all with one accord in one place.*

Acts 2:2 *And suddenly there came a sound from Heaven as of a rushing mighty wind, and it filled all the house where they were sitting.* Please continue reading **Acts 2:3-4** to have a complete background of this event:

Acts 2:5 *And there were dwelling at Jerusalem, devout men, out of every nation under Heaven.*

At Pentecost: The outpouring of the Holy Spirit of Christ was fulfilled. **John 14:16, 26; 15:26; 16:7.** The Holy Spirit are the cells of the Body of Christ or the bread of life which He gave up for the remission of our Sins at Calvary. We have to eat of this bread.

The New Body of Christ

Baptism by the Holy Spirit of every believer in Jerusalem took place. The Bible also calls this the Comforter, Helper and Counselor or Paraclete. Thus, the union between human spirit and the Holy Spirit of Christ form the **New Body of Jesus Christ.** And the gathering of the sheep unto Christ has begun. We have a **New Infant Jesus Christ or Santo Nino.** Virgin Mary is taking care of this Holy Child in every step of His way until He grows up to be a grown man named Jesus Christ. I believe this is the reason why so many early Catholic Churches were named after her.

What constitute the Body of Christ for His Second Advent?

Every time, a person accepts Jesus Christ as Lord and Savior and Him Crucified; with a contrite heart, a blood covenant occurs: the heart is cut or opened and blood is shed, likewise with the shed blood of Jesus at Calvary, allows the Holy Spirit to enter the heart of man. Apostle Paul calls this, the circumcision of the heart. Also known as baptism by the Holy Spirit said by John the Baptist. When this spiritual event takes place, the in dwelling of the Holy Spirit into the heart of a believer is now a done deal.

At the Feast of Pentecost, as the outpouring of the Holy Spirit into this world took place as promised by Christ to His Disciples, manifested by speaking tongues. At the same time, the union of the human spirit (Man)/believer or church and of the Holy Spirit (Jesus Christ) has begun to gather to form the **Body of Christ.** And every time, a man accepts and declares that Christ is his Lord and Savior, a family comprised of man as head, wife and children (formed as cell) adds another cell to the **Body of Christ.** The spiritual Body will grow from a baby again. This baby Jesus is composed of the early saints and I believe also included are the Old Testament saints. Please note that it is similar to when Christ was born as a baby in a manger in His First Advent.

A **Believer or Church** is now grafted in Jesus Christ as the True Vine (John 15:1). Therefore the **Body of Christ** will grow, **one spiritual cell at a time.** To further clarify; a Spiritual cell that forms the Spiritual Body of Christ can be explained as the union of Holy Spirit (Spirit of God, the Father and the Son Jesus Christ – one cell of the Body of Christ in the flesh) and human spirit cell (a human family cell-the spirit of husband and wife + some children combined). I also believe, all the Old Testament Saints at Pentecost will receive the Holy Spirit together with the living New Testament Saints at that time. Together they will comprise the **Body of Christ**. Jews and Gentile Christians are now one as brothers and sisters. There is no more distinction between the two groups. **We can picture it as the Kingdom of God, Matt. 6:33.**

I believe this is one of the main reasons, why it is taking Lord Jesus Christ long in coming back. All we are told; it is soon. For the time being: we must, just be grateful and thankful that He (Jesus) came, and that the Father called us to accept Christ, as His Son. **Being a member of the Body of Christ is the best thing that could ever happen to any man.**

Spiritual Act:

We believers becomes one family with our Father in Heaven and this is the reason we can ask of anything and everything we need to live this life in this worldly Earth.

God made man to be rich in Him. He did not create us to live in poverty and in misery. **God Loves Us. John 3:16**

Why is the Church, has the Spirit of a Man and Man as Head?

1 Cor. 11:3 *But I would have you know, that the head of every man is Christ; and the head of the woman is the man; and the Head of Christ is God.* When the man (husband) makes Christ and Him Crucified as the focus of his faith, the wife and rest of the family are also sanctified. **Acts 16:31-34** ... *Believe on the Lord Jesus Christ, and you shall be saved; and your house.*

Alive in the Spirit

Rom. 8:1 *There is therefore now no condemnation to them which are in Christ Jesus, who walk not after the flesh, but after the Spirit.*

Rom. 8:2 *For the Law of the Spirit of Life in Christ Jesus has made me free from the Law of Sin and Death.*

Conduct of Women:

1 Tim. 2:9 *In like manner also, that women adorn themselves in modest apparel, with shamefacedness and sobriety; not with broided hair, or gold or pearls, or costly array.*

1 Tim. 2:10 *But, (which becomes women professing Godliness) with good works.*

1 Tim 2:12 *But I suffer not a woman to teach, nor to usurp authority over the man, but to be in silence.* Yes, a woman can teach about the Word of God, but she cannot be a Pastor (head of a congregation) or be the High Priest of the family, for this title has already been reserved for the husband or man. Husbands must learn diligently the Word of God. Pastor or High Priest authority is vested in men.

In the same manner, in the **Membership of Body of the Christ,** the husband is also the branch (cell) grafted into the Vine.

1 Tim. 2:13 *For Adam was first formed, then Eve.* This shows the order of Creation or creation model. The head of the woman is her husband, **1 Cor. 11:3.** The man has the privilege of presenting his body a living sacrifice holy and perfect to Lord Jesus.

1 Tim. 2:14 *And Adam was not deceived, but the woman being deceived was in the transgression.* Adam's eating also of the forbidden fruit completes the sin and Eve being deceived is also part of the sin. That is why both received punishment including the serpent.

1 Tim. 2:15 *Notwithstanding she shall be saved in childbearing, if they continue in Faith and Charity and Holiness with sobriety.* It is very important that the husband is a born again man in faith in Jesus and in the Father. For, he will sanctify his wife and the whole family. I believe childbearing of the wife solidifies her position as a big part of his body, because the husband will always love her and he will not cast her away (divorce her) no matter what.

Eph. 5:22 *Wives submit yourselves unto your own husbands, as unto the Lord.* It is only profitable for the wife to submit to the husband if he has received Christ and is a **Member of the Body of Christ.**

Eph. 5:23 *For the husband is the head of the wife, even as Christ is the head of the Church: and He is the Saviour of the Body.*

Eph. 5:24 *Therefore as the Church is subject unto Christ, so let the wives be to their own husbands in everything.* These 3 above verses are only possible if the husband is a **Member of the Body of Christ.**

The Growing of the Body of Christ:

As more and more people; accepts and believes, the **Body of Christ** will keep on growing until.!!!

The last union of human spirit (Man) and the Holy Spirit (Jesus) completes the **Membership of the Body of Christ.** Then Jesus comes back for His Second Coming (Second Advent). See **Matt 24:43**

I believe Jesus' Body in His Second Coming will be as big or the same in His First Coming, as when He was Crucified

at Calvary. He gave His broken Body and shed Blood on the Passover to redeem man.

The Family is a Cell

The husband (man) is considered as the High Priest or Head of the family (cell). And Man's spirit plus the spirit of wife and children are part of his spiritual body, or human spiritual cell. If the man believes in Christ then the Holy Spirit plus, the human spirit composes the **Body of Christ.** (See **1 Cor. 11:3**). **Gen. 3:16** ... *and your desire shall be to your husband, and he shall rule over you....*

Eph. 5:28 *So ought men to love their wives as their own bodies. He who loves his wife loves himself.* The spirit of a man (male) is not complete without the female spirit (wife), therefore every man must find a wife to love. For the wife makes the man's body bigger and complete.

Eph. 5:29 *For no man ever yet hated his own flesh; but nourishes and cherishes it, even as the Lord the Church.* This verse tells us of the wedding between Jesus Christ and the Church, the Bridegroom and the Bride on the Feast of the Last Great Day.

If the family has a son, and the son takes a wife; then son will cleave to his wife. The new family becomes a new branch or cell. This is considered as spiritual cell regeneration.

Gen. 2:24 ***Therefore, shall a man leave his father and his mother, and shall cleave to his wife; and they shall be one flesh.*** Also read **Eph. 5:31**

This passage is interpreted as **family regeneration or seed multiplication. It is also equivalent to cellular regeneration of the human body** that enables it to grow from babyhood to adulthood. Since the body of man is composed of cells. **And so is the Body of Christ is also composed of Spiritual Cells.**

Therefore, it is very important that every man should secure a **Membership unto the Body of Christ** at an early age (in the 20s) and should take a wife (get married on earth as it is also in heaven). And ask God to give him a son or better more sons. So his seed can regenerate. By being secured in his membership, the man's family has the assurance of blanket protection as promised by Christ. All these seeds are called the seed of Abraham, the father of our Faith.

Also man fulfills God's command; Go and multiply. Now we know the reason why in multiplying, we must be in the **Body of Christ**. In this position, the evil one cannot destroy the family of God.

> At About.Com – Biology: And I quote "On Human Cells; it is estimated; the body of an adult man contains from **75 to 100 trillion cells.**"

If this is the quantity of cells required to compose the body of 1(one) man, then we can also say, this is also the quantity of believers required to complete the **Body of Christ**, to usher in His Second Advent.

The seeds to compose, the **Body of Christ** is as many as the dust of the Earth, is as many as the stars of the Heaven, and as the sand, which is upon the seashore.

To Abraham: **Gen 22:17** *That in blessing I will bless you, and in multiplying I will multiply your seed as the stars of the heaven, and as the sand which is upon the seashore; and your seed shall possess the gate of his enemies.* This promise to Abraham is the same promise he made to Jacob. This illustrates Our Father's consistency whenever He makes a Covenant with us. We always get impeccable assurance. God shows us and let us know that His Word, His Promise will never fail.

To Jacob: **Gen. 28:14** *And your seed shall be as the dust of the Earth, and you shall spread abroad to the west, and to the east, and to the north, and to the south: and to you and to your seed shall all the families of the Earth be blessed.*

Gen. 28:15 *And behold, I am with you, and will keep you in all places where you go, and will bring you again into this land; for I will not leave you, until I have done that which I have spoken to you of.*

Verses 14 & 15: God's promise to Jacob pertains to all believers/ seed who will become Members and comprise the **Body of Christ**. They will have the Father's blessings and protection where ever they go. The word member, seed, branch, family, and cell mean the same. See Figure 1 for better understanding and visualization of these verses.

Matt. 24:43 *But know this, that if the goodman of the house had known in what watch the thief would come, he would have watched, and would not have suffered his house to be broken up.*

Matt. 24:44 *Therefore be ye also ready: for in such an hour as you think the Son of Man cometh.* The "Goodman" here illustrates the husband, as the High Priest of the home. And he must be watchful all the time; meaning he must be spiritually anchored and his faith steadfast (like the Philadelphia Church), which is solely focused on the finished work of Jesus Christ at the Cross.

Validates that he (the branch) must be firmly grafted unto the True Vine (Jesus).

Christ's Great Commission:

In Matt. 28:19 *Go ye therefore, and teach all nations, baptizing them in the Name of the Father, and of the Son, and of the Holy Spirit:* The Great Commandment for the Church: Our job one.

Matt. 28:20 *Teaching them to observe all things whatsoever I have commanded you:* ***and lo, I am with you always, even unto the end of the world.***

The above verses are the Christ command for the Great Commission as well as a Promise of Protection as we obey His command. The promise of protection is likewise available, as we spend our lives in this world. We at the present Church, have to work to learn the Gospel of Jesus Christ, so we can bring and deliver this Good News to the whole world. So that all who has an ear let them hear. In the end they will be as we are: a **Member of the Body of Christ.**

Members of the Body of Christ

To be a **Member of the Body of Christ**, is important that we are consecrated.

Rom. 12:1 *I beseech you therefore, Brethren, by the Mercies of God; that you present your bodies a Living Sacrifice, holy, acceptable unto God, which is your reasonable service*

Rom. 12:*2 And be not conformed to this world: but be you transformed by the renewing of your mind, that you may prove what is that good, and acceptable, and Perfect, Will of God.*

Therefore, to obtain the privilege of membership unto the **Body of Jesus Christ,** one must be born again by the Grace and Mercies of God we are now a New Creation ready to present our bodies as Living Sacrifice, holy and perfect.

Rom. 12:3 *For I say, through the grace given unto me, to every man who is among you, not to think of himself more highly than he ought to think, but to think soberly; according as God has dealt to every man the **measure of faith.*** A reminder to those who has heard the Gospel of Christ and especially to them who has accepted the Gospel: Do not use it, in any manner not acceptable to God. The Holy Spirit is telling us that to be in Christ we must act in the whole context of Love.

Thus, Christ Second Commandment: **Love one another as you love yourself, and He has loved us.**

Rom. 12:4 *For as we have many members in one body, and all members have not the same office;*

Rom. 12:5 *So we, being many, are one body in Christ, and every one members one of another.*

Rom. 12:6 *Having the gifts differing according to the grace that is given to us, whether Prophecy, let us Prophesy according to the proportion of Faith*

Rom. 12:7 *Or Ministry, let us wait on our Ministering; or he who teaches, on teaching;*

Rom. 12:8 *Or he who exhorts, on exhortation: he who gives, let him do with simplicity; he who rules, with diligence; he who shows mercy, with cheerfulness.*

To summarize what verses 4-8 means is that all members must act in harmony with one another, and act as one body, as it should, whatever purpose or task each member is given according to the measure of his Faith, that is, we must be all acting on the parameters of Love.

The measure of Faith is the thirty, sixty and hundred fold blessing.
One Body:

More verses to describe the formation of the **Body of Christ.** There is no need to articulate Verses 1 Cor. 12:12-31.

1 Cor. 12:12 *For as the Body is one, and has many members, and all the members of that one Body, being many, are one Body: so also is Christ.*

1 Cor. 12:13 *For by one Spirit are we all baptized into one Body, whether we be Jews or Gentiles, whether we be bond or free; and have been all made to drink into one Spirit.*

1 Cor. 12:14 *For the Body is not one member, but many.*

1 Cor. 12:15 *If the foot shall say, because I am not the hand, I am not of the body; is it therefore not of the body?*

1 Cor. 12:16 *And if the ear shall say, because I am not the eye, Am not of the body; is it therefore not of the body?*

1 Cor. 12:17 *If the whole body were an eye, where were the hearing? If the whole were hearing, where were the smelling?*

1 Cor. 12:18 *But now has God set the members every one of them in the body, as it has pleased Him.*

1 Cor. 12:19 *And if they were all one member, where were the body?*

1 Cor. 12:20 *But now are they many members, yet but one body.*

1 Cor. 12:21 *And the eye cannot say unto the hand, I have no need of you: nor again the head to the feet, I have no need of you.*

1 Cor. 12:22 *Nay, much more those members of the body, which seem to be more feeble are necessary:*

1 Cor. 12:23 *And those members of the body, which we think to be less honorable, upon these we bestow more abundant honor; and our uncomely parts have more abundant comeliness.*

1 Cor. 12:24 *For our comely parts have no need: but God has tempered the body together, having given more abundant honour to that part which lacked:*

1 Cor. 12:25 *That there should be no schism in the body: but that the members should have the same care one for another.*

1 Cor. 12:26 *And whether one member suffer, all the members suffer with it; or one member be honoured, all the members rejoice with it.*

! Cor. 12:27 *Now ye are the body of Christ, and members in particular.*

1 Cor. 12:28 *And God has set some in the church, first apostles, secondarily prophets, thirdly teachers, after that miracles, then gifts of healing, helps, governments, diversities of tongues.*

1 Cor. 12:29 *Are all apostles? Are all prophets? Are all teachers? Are all workers of miracles?*

1 Cor. 12:30 *Have all the gifts of healing? Do all speak with tongues? Do all interpret?*

1 Cor. 12:31 *But covet earnestly the best gifts: and yet show you a more excellent way.*

There could be no place for hate, or division among the members, if we are to be in the **Body of Christ**. If a member brings hate into the Body, surely he will be cut off. Read **John 15:1** The Husbandman or Vinedresser (Our Father in Heaven) is always tending the Vine. It also means that although we are still alive in our corrupted flesh, we the believers are now grafted branches unto the **Body of Christ**.

We may still be in this world, but we are living not of this world. And the cares of this world, we set them aside, and don't worry about them; "Matt 6:33. Seek ye first the Kingdom of God..." The old man has to die. (Old self or leave our Egypt behind)

This is the perfect illustration of living a holy spiritual life, while still alive in the flesh and bones. Now that we have an idea on how to truly live for God, let us examine our whole spiritual being if we have that **Spiritual Wellness** that we all must desire. That is **First and Foremost.**

Spiritual Wellness vs. Health (flesh and bones) Wellness

Spiritual Wellness is more than a zillion times needed by man rather than Physical Health Wellness (of the corrupted human body).

Why so? Man was not created to live in the corrupted flesh and bones forever. When man was first created, Adam and Eve have glorified bodies they are covered with white, destined to live forever with their Creator God.

Then sin entered into the lives of man and all broke loose. God said, now it is appointed unto man once to die. Why did God, did that? So God can claim His most prized creation back on certain appointed time when the Kingdom Age can be instituted again, at the Second Advent of Christ.

What is Spiritual Wellness?

Our spiritual condition that we gather in the presence of Jesus Christ, being able to commune with Him. He said, we are not His servants, but rather His friends and brothers. And most of all, we are Insiders in His Kingdom. Actually, I believe that we also wine and dine with our Master in Heaven. We are in His comfort zone, so to speak.

In His Kingdom there will be no more sickness, problems, and misery. All the things we hope to have while we are still in flesh. Actually we can have it in this life of flesh and bones, if only we will not worry about dying in our first death. We should experience a calm peace, if we are in Christ and Him in us or we are in the Body of Christ.

Therefore, how do we obtain Spiritual Wellness? Cheerfully accept, confess with your mouth and Believes in Jesus Christ as our Lord and Saviour and Him Crucified. I believe when you speak these words you are born again and becomes a **Member of the Body of Christ**. God's free gift of Grace and Mercy is upon you. Thus you don't have to spend millions of dollars.

Now compare the Spiritual Wellness to Physical Health Wellness.

When we get sick our first impulse is to get the best doctor, best hospital available and most expensive. Thinking we will get well, but sometimes it works and sometimes it doesn't. The end result is always the same. We all die. So, why would I prefer physical wellness?

In my view, it is a million times better to just donate the money intended for lavish medical procedures to a local Bible based Church or to foundations feeding and improving the lives of the poor. Or simply save 50% of it for your relatives struggling to make ends meet.

Only a suggestion, but don't leave out your local Church. We are to obey Jesus' Commandment to spread His Gospel to the ends of the Earth. "The Great Commission," Man's job one.

I have known someone who was diagnosed with lung cancer at an early age of 30 years old. She didn't smoke and she did not drink hard wine. But she got sick early in life anyway. She did not bother to go through all the chemo- therapy and medications prescribed by her doctor and preferred to live in peace. Spent money only to control her pain. She just started eating right, a little exercise daily, a happy demeanor day in day out and indulge in the things she loved to do. She lived for 5 more years and she made sure she has Jesus Christ on her side. This we can say we are in the best place after death. Absolutely resting in peace. It is wrong to say that when someone dies that they are in a better place. It is not true. It will only be true if the one who dies has Christ dwelling in their hearts.

Spiritual War

Eph 6:10 *Finally, my brethren, be strong in the Lord, and in the power of His Might.*

Eph. 6:11 *Put on the **whole Armor of God**, that you maybe able to stand against the wiles of the Devil.*

Eph. 6:12 *For we wrestle not against flesh and blood; but against principalities, against powers, against the rulers of darkness of this world, against spiritual wickedness in high places.*

Our main enemy in this earth; are not our fellow man, but evil principalities not only on face of earth but up there in high places where Satan has also established his kingdom. Although Satan was defeated at Calvary; he has not been removed yet from his stronghold position. Therefore, we must always be in the **Body of Christ,** He is our "whole Armor of God" put Him on for our protection 24/7/365.

That's why we need to become **Members of the Body of Christ.** Being an insider, we have total protection. Satan cannot attack Christ.

True Christians: The Israel of God Today.

Isaiah 58:1 *Cry aloud, spare not, lift up your voice like a trumpet, and show My people their transgression, and the house of Jacob their sins.*

Although we have received Christ as Lord and Savior, we are still sinners. The temptation and cares of this world is hard to overcome falling unto sin every now and then, but we also know that by seeking our God, we can ask for forgiveness and cleansing of our iniquities.

Isaiah 58:2 *Yet they seek Me daily, and delight to know My Ways, as a nation that did righteousness, and forsook not the ordinances of their God, they ask of Me the ordinances of justice, they take delight* *in approaching to God.* To seek God daily puts us back to the fold of our Lord Jesus Christ, and this is the only way for us Church to be grafted always to the True Vine.

To be outside the **Body of Christ,** we do not have protection from the thief, the killer and the destroyer and deceiver. Remember his attributes all the time. So we can avoid being tempted and forever be destroyed. **We are free game for Satan, if Christ is not in us.** We cannot defeat him on our own.

The gathering of Nations, Family (spiritual cell), and Abraham seeds, and the Holy Spirit to grow the **Body of Christ.**

Matt. 25:32 *And before Him shall he gather all nations; and He shall separate them from one another, as a shepherd divides His sheep from the goats.*

We can only defeat Satan, if Christ is with us to do the battle for us. He is God Immanuel.

What shall we do to keep Satan away?

Pray every day, to maintain our spiritual connection to our Father through Christ. Do not allow him to deceive you again. Wear the Armor of God, the Body of Christ. Never listen to things that are too good to be true. Reject his temptations at all cost and at all times. Keep grounded in the Word of God to secure a **Membership in the Body of Christ.**

CHAPTER 22

The Blessings

Membership's Unlimited Privileges: God Rewards for Obedience

To the believers, the Church, great rewards are waiting for them in Heaven. Just imagine you are spending your eternal life with your Father in Heaven. Imagine how wonderful it is to be with your Creator. Not enough words to describe it.

You see, Our Father in Heaven employs a reward system, just like our biological father on earth also will give us anything we ask from him no matter what! How much more will our Father in Heaven give us. His will in Heaven is just the same as His will on Earth. "Give us this day our daily bread" We just have to ask for it daily. That means we have to pray every day. We can also ask for the desires of our heart. Read the Lord's Prayer or some say the believers' prayer. **Matthew 6:9-15**

Eph. 3:20 *Now unto Him Who is able to do exceeding abundantly above all that we ask or think, according to the power that works in us.* The last phrase "according . . ." refers to what the Holy Spirit can do in us, by how much is the measure of our Faith in Christ Jesus; will it be 30, 60, or 100 fold.

We can also call this as; God's prescribed Order of Victory generated by Christ's Finished Work on the Cross at Calvary.

Eph. 3:21 *Unto Him be Glory in the Church by Christ Jesus* (**Body of Christ**) *throughout all ages, world without end. Amen.* Eternal Kingdom.

Hope in Christ:

Heb. 6:13 *For; when God made Promise to Abraham, because He could swear by no greater, He swore by Himself.*

Heb. 6:14 *Saying, Surely blessing I will bless you, and multiplying I will multiply you.* Please continue reading Heb. 6:15-16

Heb. 6:17 *Wherein God, willing more abundantly to show unto the heirs of Promise the immutability of His counsel, confirmed it by an oath.*

Heb. 6:18 *That by two immutable things, in which it was impossible for God to lie, we might have a strong consolation, who have fled for refuge to lay hold upon the hope set before us.* Trust in the Lord, and not lean on our own understanding

Heb. 6:19 *Which hope we have as an anchor of the soul, both sure and steadfast; and which enters into that within the Veil.* Portrays the throne of our Heavenly Father, before Christ crucifixion.

Heb. 6:20 *Whither the Forerunner is for us entered, even Jesus, made a High Priest forever after the order of Melchizedec.* This pertains to, when God's Feast of the Great Day of Atonement will take place after the Feast of Trumpets has come to pass. When Christ as our High Priest will enter into the Most Holy Place of God to intercede and atone for our sins and all the sins of the world for all time. The verse also confirms that Christ as the Second Adam has the title of Eternal High Priest in the order of Melchizedec, which means it has no end or forever interceding for man's sin.

Wisdom

Prov. 8:1 *Does not wisdom cry? And understanding put forth her voice?* Wisdom is personified as the Word of God. And to understand the True Gospel brings the true nature of God in the open.

Prov. 8:3 *She cries at the gates, at the entry of the city, at the coming at the doors.* The Holy Spirit is seeking us at every opportunity, to put forth the Word of God and be heard by men; so that we may be saved for God so loved the world.

Prov. 8:4 *Unto you, O men, I call, and my voice is to the sons of man.* The Holy Spirit is calling all, old and young men alike to hear the voice or Word of God. God's calling is only for men, not to any other of God's creation, like angels and animals.

Prov. 8:5 *O you simple, understand wisdom, and you fools, be you of an understanding heart.* Humble men have simple ways and they are the ones who have wisdom to believe the Word of God, and the learned are fools for they reject the Word of God and must re-new their hearts and minds to believe.

Prov. 8:6 *Hear, for I will speak of excellent things: and the opening of my lips shall be right things.* Says that God does not make mistakes, so we better heed His Words for we are assured that they will benefit us with mighty things.

Prov. 8:7 *For my mouth shall speak truth, and wickedness is an abomination to my lips.* Only speak the words with value and truth.

Prov. 8:8 *All the words of my mouth are in Righteousness; there is nothing froward or perverse in them.* By God's wisdom, we follow Gods' words in the Bible, He will led us to the **Body of Christ, our desired destination.**

Prov. 8:9 *They are all plain to him who understands, and right to them who find knowledge.* The word of God is very Profitable in every way. Please read Prov. 8:10-11

Prov. 8:12 *I wisdom dwell with prudence, and find out knowledge of witty inventions.* This verse on wisdom answers my question: base on a research presented by Grant Jeffrey in his TV program ""Bible Prophecy Revealed", he said that 75 to 80% of major inventions and discoveries in science and technology were made by Christians (Gentiles and Jews) and Jews. Why? God reveals His wisdom to those that believes and listens to Him.

Prov. 8:13 *The fear of the Lord is to hate evil: pride, and arrogance, and the evil way and the froward mouth, do I hate.* This verse gives us the real meaning of fear of the Lord.

Prov. 8:14 *Counsel is mine, and sound wisdom, I am understanding: I have strength.* In all our problems there is only one counselor we have to go to. Come to Jesus.

Prov. 8:15 *By me kings reign, and princes decree justice.* The Head of a nation can command Satan to leave his country in order that a country can prosper. The same is also true with the Church or believer for they are empowered to rule and reign in this world with Christ. We can speak the Word of God to tell our holy guardian angels to prosper us, heal sickness, solve our problems and cast away evil around us. If Satan is not cast away he can prevent progress to take root.

Prov. 8:16 *By me princes rule, and nobles, even all the judges of the Earth.* God empowers head of nations, but if they are corrupt, He can take away the blessings, therefore the citizens will suffer especially if corruption is rampant.

Prov. 8:17 *I love them who love me, and those that seek me early shall find me.* Teach our children: Who is Jesus Christ: especially the boys, that they understand there is a true God we need to obey. So that they know their role in the family, that he has the privilege to be High Priest of the house someday.

Prov. 8:18 *Riches and honour are with me, yes, durable riches and righteousness.* Durable riches are those treasures we keep in Heaven. Where, it cannot be destroyed; by moth and other elements.

Prov. 8:19 *My fruit is better than gold, yes, than fine gold; and my revenue than choice silver.* The fruit we must bear are those derived from our faith and Love. Without faith we cannot please God.

Examples of durable fruits or riches: a) fruit of the womb, b) teaching the Gospel of Christ to friends, relatives and neighbors and results in the acceptance of the Gospel, c) loving and lifting up one another, by doing these we feel God's love for us, d) offering love gifts and thanksgiving to the Lord. There are many more that we can think of, which is good to all.

Prov. 8:20 *I lead in the way of righteousness, in the midst of the paths of judgment.* Even if we are living in this world, we are not a citizen of this world, we live in a world of the Holy Spirit, where, we are not bound to be judged. We live in a world without condemnation, in Christ Jesus.

Prov. 8:21 *That I may cause those who love me to inherit substance, and I will fill their treasures.* To those who loved God, becomes **Members of the Body of Christ.** Or we can say becomes a part of the Family of God. This is why the promises of God are fulfilled in them. My concern is why people still wants to opposed God, wherein Satan's promises cannot be relied upon. They are not durable.

In summary: If we hear the voice of the Holy Spirit giving us instructions on the Word of God, we will gain wisdom; the wisdom to be a **Member of the Body of Christ.** Thus becoming an insider in the Kingdom of God, God will give us anything we will ask from Him. **Prov. 8:21** says it all. Wisdom is everlasting,

Heirs to Rule and Reign:

We are more than conquerors of our enemies, but more than that. We are Heirs of the Most High God in His Kingdom, we rule and reign with Christ.

Rom. 8:14 *For as many as led by the Spirit of God, they are Sons of God.* We are led; by the Spirit of God to the Cross of Christ, to become Sons of God, if we accept and believe, we are **Members of the Body of Christ.**

Rom. 8:15 *For you have not received the spirit of bondage* (spirit of sin), *again to fear; but you have receive the Spirit of Adoption, whereby we cry Abba, Father.*

When we repent of our sins and reject Satan, we receive Jesus, then the Holy Spirit will adopt us into the Family of God or **Body of Christ.**

Rom. 8:16 *The Spirit itself bears witness with our spirit, that we are the Children of God.* The Holy Spirit and our spirit are together. There is an in-dwelling between the Spirits and Abba, Father delights in the union and calls us Children of God.

Rom. 8:17 *And if Children, then heirs; heirs of God, and joint heirs with Christ; if so be that we suffer with Him, that we may be also glorified.*

Heb. 1:2 *Has in the last days spoken unto us by His Son, Whom He has appointed Heir of all things, by Whom also He made the worlds.*

Col. 1:18 *And He is the Head of the Body, the Church; Who is the beginning, the Firstborn from the dead; that in all things He might have the preeminence.*

Col. 1:19 *For it pleased the Father that in Him should all fullness dwell.* Verse 18 says: Jesus the head of the **Body of Christ,** which is composed of the Holy Spirit and the Church.

Eph. 2:6 *And raised us up together, and made us sit together in Heavenly Places in Christ Jesus.* When Christ was resurrected from death or tomb, together we are also resurrected with Him as well through **our Faith** in Him.

Thereby, He also brought us to dwell in His Kingdom in Heaven or the Body of Christ or Paradise. These are the Heavenly places this verse is talking about.

Rupture: Protection for True Christians

Here is Christ's warning to His Church to escape the coming Great Tribulation.

Luke 21:34 *And take heed to yourselves, lest at any time your hearts be overcharged with surfeiting, and drunkenness, and cares of this life, and so that day come upon you unawares.* Jesus is telling us; do not over indulged in whatever pleasure this world can give, that we will forget Him and or else we will be cut off from the True Vine. **John 15:1.** We must not be caught unaware of the Vine dressing by Our Father.

Jesus is teaching us to watch and pray that we will not be caught unaware of His return. Or else we miss the boat ride.

The Holy Feast of the Trumpets or at Rupture

1 Thess. 4:13 *But I would not have you to be ignorant, Brethren, concerning them which are asleep, that you sorrow not, even as others which have no hope.* Those who died in the flesh without Christ have no hope to be in Paradise, **Very Clear**.

1 Thess. 4:14 *For if we believe that Jesus died and rose again, even so them also which sleep in Jesus will God bring with Him.* We are able to follow Christ, wherever He goes if we are members of His Body.

1 Thess. 4:16 *For the Lord Himself shall descend from Heaven with a shout, with the voice of the Archangel and with the Trump of God: and the dead in Christ shall rise first.*

1 Thess. 4:17 *Then; we, which are alive and remain shall be caught up together with them in the clouds to meet the Lord in the air: and so shall ever be with the Lord arrives.* Upon the sound of the trumpet, the **Members of the Body of Christ,** will be **met by Jesus in the clouds** including those who are still alive and saved. The unsaved will be left behind, to endure the Great Tribulations.

1 Cor. 15:51 *Behold, I show you a mystery; we will not all sleep, but we shall all be changed.* At Rupture, many Christians will be alive (Resurrected) even the dead in Christ.

1 Cor. 15:52 *In a moment, in the twinkling of an eye, at the last trump: for the trumpet shall sound, and the dead shall be raised* *incorruptible, and we shall be changed.* We will put on a **Glorified Body.** The same body that Adam and Eve has before she was tempted and sin entered into the lives of man.

1 Cor. 15:53 *For this corruptible must put on incorruption, and this mortal must put on immortality.* At this time, our flesh and bones has shed away its sin nature and now our spirit possess a glorified body; immortality or eternal life.

We are now ready to enter into the **Kingdom of God.** Next the Feast of the Tabernacles will take place.

Watch and Pray:

Luke 21:35 *For as a snare shall it come on all them who dwell on the face of the whole earth.* For the left behind, there is no escape from the tribulation, but to endure. Anyone who is in his right mind will not wish to be in a horrible situation such as the Great Tribulation. There will be no comfort zone for anyone.

See Luke 21:24 *"And they shall fall by the edge of the sword and shall be led away captive into all nations, and Jerusalem shall be trodden down of the Gentiles, until the times of the Gentiles be fulfilled*

Luke 21:36 *Watch ye therefore, and pray always, that you maybe accounted worthy to escape all these things that shall come to pass, and to stand before the Son of Man.* If we remain vigilant in our Faith in Christ and maintain our position as grafted branch into the **Body of Christ**, we are assured to stand before the Son of Man.

See 1 Tess. 5:2 *"For yourselves know perfectly that the Day of the Lord so comes as a thief in the night.*

1 Thess. 5:4 *But you, Brethren, are not in darkness, that that day should overtake you as a thief"*

The verse above says: that all must become true Christians and must always be in a state of spiritual readiness. No one must wait until later to Repent and Obey God's Commandments.

If you accept Jesus as your Lord and Saviour, you already obeyed God's Commandments. Our Father sees you as His Son.

Let us validate the above statements with the following verses:

John 14:1 *Let not your heart be troubled: you believe in God, believe also in Me.* Jesus talking to comfort us.

John 14:7 *If you had known me, you should have known my Father also; and from Henceforth you know Him, and have seen Him.* Once we know Jesus we know the Father

John 14:9 *... He who has seen me has seen the Father.* Father and Son are One, One in Spirit.

Isaiah 41:10 ***Fear you not;*** *for I am with you: be not dismayed; for I am your God. I will strengthen you; yes, I will help you, yea. I will uphold you with the right hand of My Righteousness.* God guarantees our victory against our enemies if we are **Members of the Body of Christ.**

Provision:

John 14:12 *Verily, verily, I say unto you. He who believes in Me, the works that I do shall he do also: and greater Works than these shall he do; because I go into my Father.* I believe, once we get our glorified Body back, we can do what Jesus did, like feeding the multitude of more that 5000 people by blessing only 5 loaves of bread and 2 fishes.

John 14:13 *And whatsoever you shall ask in my name, that I will do, that the Father maybe glorified in the Son.* There is no need to worry about anything, because God will provide. Review Matt. 6:25-35

John 14:14 *If you shall ask anything in my name, I will do it.* How do we know that God is talking to us or letting us know what is His will for us?

Answer: God will talk to us in the same manner that He has spoken to Moses, to the Prophets and to His Apostles. If we are **Members of the Body of Christ,**

God will surely speak to us via dreams, visions, in His still small voice, revelations and events in our lives that is designed to catch our attention or force us to do something and it does not give us any alternative or option to do anything else. Similar to what happened to Jonah.

Therefore we must be adept, observant and be able to recognize that it is our beloved Jesus that is communicating.

Knowing what is God's will for us is crucial to the increase of our faith, so that we can glorify Him. Once we know what is His will, we must meditate on it and ask for wisdom how to go and do it. He will not give us an assignment that we cannot accomplish. You will be surprised, that once you started to act on your assigned work, you will be amazed how easy it is.

God's will for us could be new discoveries, inventions, new business paradigm or something really spectacular endeavor. We must be on the lookout for amazing things to happen. We cannot slumber. Or else the thief might come and destroys our hope and dreams.

Then the Vinedresser comes and we will be cut-off from the vine.

God's Complete Blessing:

When we lack of nothing, we can say we have all the Blessings that God can provide to His children. Remember, we are Father God's children, if we have Christ' in-dwelling in our Hearts. This means:

We are:

- a) Blessed Spiritually (we have Spiritual Wellness or eternal life),
- b) Physically Healthy (we are not sickly or no known serious illness even up to our old age),
- c) Profound Financial Resource (abundance of material wealth)
- d) Blessed with Wisdom and Knowledge

e) Highly Honored and with Integrity (recognized and perceived as a good man by the community where he lives)

f) Happy and there is joy in our hearts all the time. Some say: you have an extra spring in your step.

g) Blessed with a congregation that lift our spirits up and there exist a wholesome fellowship with one another and with Jesus.

h) Completely happy with the blessings we receive from God.

i) Almost immune to problems, pain and sorrow. Sickness will not be a problem, for it is our way out of this sinful world.

If we almost have all of the above, even without riches on earth, it is a good indication that you are a **Member of the Body of Christ**. Now if you only have riches, please be concerned of your Spiritual Wellness. Chances are you have not fully committed your body and spirit to God through Christ. You have not fully accepted Christ Jesus as your Lord and Savior.

God's Grace and Mercy:

Exodus 33:19 *And He said, I will make my Goodness pass before you, and I will proclaim the name of the Lord before you, and will be gracious to whom I will be gracious, and will show mercy on whom I will show mercy.*

Psalm 37:4 *Delight yourself also in the Lord; and He shall give you the desires of your heart.*

Proverbs 16:20 *He who handles a matter wisely shall find good: and whoso trust the Lord, happy is he.*

Matthew 9:29 *Then touched He their eyes, saying according to your Faith: be it unto you.* The blessing comes by the Law of ones Faith. Without Faith it is impossible to please God. Without Faith God blessings cannot flow to them who desires it or ask for it. For God is good.

Matthew 18:19 *Again I say unto you, that if two of you shall agree on earth as touching anything that they shall ask, it shall be done for them of my Father which is in Heaven.* A good example of this is: when a man and a woman professes love for one another and agree to get married, then God will perform their marriage on Earth and in Heaven. Any High Priest on Earth can perform the marriage on Earth. The State should not get involve in this.

How about same sex union? If the people of a State unanimously approved a law for such union, they can get approval only on Earth from people who are not in the **Truth.** I don't believe it will be done in Heaven because it violates the Laws of God. This type of union does not profit God nor does it profit man. Of course, God will allow it because of man's free will but **He will not recognize it as marriage**, no matter how much you spin your wheels for those who wants it, for it does not fit God's definition. So why still do it. Anything we do that does not fit God's word is an opposition to God and a waste. Therefore be aware, for vengeance is His. Rom. 12:19.

Philippians 4:6 *Rejoice in the Lord always: and again I say Rejoice.*

Galatians 6:9 *And let us not be weary in well doing for in due season we shall reap, if we faint not.* The Lord's blessing will come to pass on appointed time, let us not give up on expecting what He has promised us.

While waiting keep on sowing a seed, learn God's Seed Principle. Sowing a seed validates our faith.

Rupture: "This word might not be in the Holy Bible but it best describe the events that will take place in **1 Thess. 4:13-17**". Anyone, who wants to be left behind?

The Beatitudes:

Matt. 5:3 *Blessed are the poor in spirit: for theirs is the Kingdom of Heaven.* The Kingdom of Heaven is always present in the spiritual realm in the Heavenly places. Entry to this Kingdom is now assured only thru faith in Christ Jesus. When He was present physically on earth, He is the Kingdom of God. At present we have access to this kingdom by virtue of our **Membership in the Body of Christ.** "Poor in Spirit" means we humbled our self to Christ and we believed Him as Lord. Or when we come to Christ just like **babes.**

Matt. 5:4 *Blessed are they who mourn: for they shall be comforted.* To the believers who wept and felt sorry they sinned against God and their brothers and sisters. Christ will comfort us through the work of the Holy Spirit, which is also He.

Matt. 5:5 *Blessed are the meek: for they shall inherit the earth.*

Matt. 5:6 *Blessed are they which do hunger and thirst after Righteousness: for they shall be filled.* Christ will satisfy all our spiritual and material needs while still living in this world for we will be **Members of the Body of Christ.**

Matt. 5:7 *Blessed are the merciful: for they shall obtain mercy.*

Matt. 5:8 *Blessed are the pure in heart: for they shall see God.*

Matt. 5:9 *Blessed are the peacemakers: for they shall be called the Children of God.*

Matt. 5:10 *Blessed are they which are persecuted for righteousness sake: for theirs is the Kingdom of Heaven.*

Matt. 5:11 *Blessed are you, when men shall revile you, and persecute you, and shall say all manners of evil against you falsely, for My sake.* This is exactly what Muslims falsely accuse the Jews and Christians: that they are infidels and deserve death. In the first place who is allah? What miracles has he done, to declare himself that he is great? We Jews and Christians are not infidels, we believe in the one true God. This is only to defend my faith that my Lord Jesus is the Most High God.

Just to clear the deception once again. I believe the Quran is a tool of Evil to deceive and kill people, including my Arab brothers as the # 1 victims. Its believers are true Muslims, the worst infidels. They believe that it is holy to hate and swear to kill all Jews and Christians to erase the Israeli nation from existence. How can anyone be holy for murder in the name allah. This cannot be denied for it is written in their books and media. Their zest to hate and kill all Jews and Christians is exactly the character of Prince Satan. It promotes hate, coercion and violence. When they claim that it is a religion of peace, beware it is a deception. In spite of all their despicable acts, they still have the potential to be my brothers that I must love and respect.

I know someday my God may call them and He may convert them to be believers in Jesus Christ instead. There is hope for all, Christ died and finished His work to redeem all. No one will be sent by God to duplicate Christ's work for it is finished. True Christians are commanded to bring the message of the Gospel of Grace and Love of Christ to the whole world. Conversion of unbelievers is the work of the Holy Spirit not man.

Matt. 5:12 *Rejoice, and be exceedingly glad: for great is your reward in Heaven: for so persecuted they the Prophets before you.* We must express our gratitude to our Father for the blessings we receive from Him, by giving our tithes and offerings and glorifying His name in all things we do.

CHAPTER 23

Giving and Thanksgiving

As a **Member of the Body of Christ**, we are expected by God to be obedient to His commandment to give to the works of God on Earth and to things of God like the poor or less fortunate, to lift up one another. God wants us to feel His love. If we give to one another, we make them feel (our fellow man) that God loves them. In return; we must give thanks and praise the Lord. By giving, we glorify Him who provides us with everything we need every day.

The American people are the most generous in the whole world. One reason we remain a blessed nation even with our horrible sin of aborting our unborn babies. But we are paying for it now.

The following verses will make us understand the importance of giving. To be in the **Body of Christ**, we must know how to give or plant a seed. We will reap what we sow.

Acts 20:35 *I have showed you all things, how that so labouring you ought to support the weak, and to remember the Words of the Lord Jesus, how He said: it is more blessed to give than to receive.* Be an example to be a cheerful giver. Once we give, we don't look back and think about it. Then we will not feel the weight. We just rejoice in the Lord.

Proverbs 28:27 *He who gives unto the poor shall not lack: but he who hides his eyes shall have many a curse.* God, will always double what you gave to the less fortunate. As we give, we store our treasures in Heaven.

King David saying: **1 Chronicles 29:3** *Moreover, because I have set my affection to the House of my God, I have of my own proper good, of gold and silver, which I have given to the House of my God, over and above all that I have prepared for the Holy House.* King David loves God. We must love God too.

1 Chronicles 29:12 *Both riches and honour come of You, and You reign over all; and in Your hand is power and might; and in Your hand it is to make great, and to give strength unto all.*

1 Chronicles 29:13 *Now therefore, Our God, we thank You, and praise Your glorious Name.*

1 Chronicles 29:14 *But who am I, and what is my people, that we should be able to offer so willingly after this sort? For all things come of You, and of Your own have we given You.*

Matthew 19:21 *Jesus said unto him, If you will be perfect, go and sell that you have, and give to the poor, and you shall have treasure in Heaven: and come and follow Me.*

Luke 21:4 *For all these have their abundance cast in unto the offerings of God: but she (*The widow with two mites*) of her penury has cast in all the living that she had.*

By God's meaning of giving: Her two mites is more valuable than those of rich men, because she gave her all. It is similar to when we follow Christ that we give our all. Abraham is our example.

Malachi 3:10 *Bring ye all the tithes into the storehouse, that there may be meat in mine house, and prove me now henceforth, saith the Lord of Hosts, if I will not open you the windows of Heaven, and there shall not be room enough to receive it.*

"tithe" is giving 10% of our net income to the Lord of Host (our Father in Heaven). This means that this is the amount we give to our local churches, which we join into a congregation of believers (church). This is the prescribed amount for giving before Christ's first advent. Even Abraham was giving tithes to the High Priest of Salem, Melchizedek. Therefore this admonition of God to the Israelites around 500 years before Christ came was not something new. Apparently, the Jewish people forgot all about giving to the Lord. So they are reminded this time.

This also shows us how important it is not to neglect our tithes and love offerings to our Father. We have to sow a seed to reap what we sow.

If we give to the Lord, here is our reward; Malachi 3:11 *And I will rebuke the devourer for your sakes, and he shall not destroy the fruits of your ground; neither shall your vine cast her fruit before the time in the field, saith the Lord of Hosts.*

Malachi 3: 12 *And all nations shall call you blessed: for ye shall be a delightsome land. Saith the Lord of Hosts.*

Matthew 5:42 *Give to him who asks of you, and from him who would borrow of you turn not you away.*

I believe this pertains to those who are sincerely in need, and not who just wants to manipulate the giver or perennial borrower. And those who are actually lazy and would not work do not deserve to eat. Read also: **II Thess. 3:10.**

Notes:

Imagine: You picture God who is in Heaven looking down on His planetary Creations; He sees the Earth, third rock from the Sun as His Headquarters in the Universe. That is, where Jesus is building His Church. Read **Matt. 16:18-19** Jesus gives the keys of the Kingdom of Heaven to all believers or **Members of the Body of Christ**. The key is a symbol of authority to preach the Word of God to the whole world.

To write this book is a big privilege for me. I could have not done this without the power of the Holy Spirit that gave me the courage and the strength. I love my Lord Jesus Christ.

CHAPTER 24

Commands and Conduct

The Members of the Body of Christ
are expected to behave and act like Christ.

1) **Commands**

Rom. 12:9 *Let love be without dissimulation. Abhor that which is evil; cleave to what is good.*

Whenever we tell someone that we love them, we make sure that it is a sincere feeling and it is truly coming from our hearts, because that love we share is coming from God. Every time we love our fellowman, we glorify our Lord Jesus.

Romans 12:10 *Be kindly affectioned one to another with brotherly love, in honor preferring one another.* As Member of the Body of Christ, we must love one another as brothers and sisters.

Romans 12:11 *Not slothful in business; fervent in Spirit; serving the Lord:*

Romans 12:12 *Rejoicing in hope; patient in tribulation; continuing instant in prayer;*

Romans 2:13 *Distributing to the necessity of Saints; given to hospitality;*

Romans 12:14 *Bless them which persecute you; bless and curse not.*

If we bless the one who persecute and curse us, their persecution and cursing will be of no effect on us and it will go back to them, because we take no part in it.

Romans 12:15 *Rejoice with them who do rejoice, and weep with them who weep.* Comfort those who need to feel God's Love.

Romans 12:16 *Be of the same mind one toward another. Mind not high things, but condescend to men of low estate. Be not wise in your own conceits.*

In the membership, there should be no conflict in the minds or interpretation of the Gospel. Do not be consumed with materialism. Humble our selves to one another. Do not manipulate of anything to profit only our self and take advantage of others.

1 Tim. 4:13 *Till I come, give attendance to reading, to exhortation, to doctrine.* While we wait and continue proclaim Christ's death on the Cross, Let us not forget to continue reading, proclaiming the Truth and the Gospel of Love, and teaching the Word of God to our children and the whole world.

1 Tim. 4:14 *Neglect not the Gift that is in you, which was given to you by Prophecy, with the laying on the hands of the Presbytery.*

1 Tim.4:15 *Meditate upon these things; give yourself wholly to them; that your profiting may appear to all.*

1 Tim. 4:16 *Take heed unto yourself, and unto Doctrine; continue in them; for in doing this you shall both save yourself, and them who hear you.*

2) **Prescribed Conduct of Members**

Rom. 12:17 *Recompense to no man evil for evil. Provide things honest in the sight of all men.*

Rom. 12:18 *If it be possible, as much as lieth in you, live peaceably with all men.*

Rom 12:19 *Dearly beloved, avenge not yourselves, but rather give place unto wrath for it is written,* **Vengeance is mine, I will repay, saith the Lord.**

Vengeance Explained:

We must not take action against our fellow man, because he may be one of your brothers or sisters in the **Body of Christ** later, but rather leave it to God's wrath. Because if we exact vengeance, we will only hurt our fellowmen, we do not have the power to hurt or punish the evil spirit who tempted man to do trespass against us. We must bless those wronged us, and God will bless us.

Whereas; God is the only one who can punish both the evil spirit and the errant man. Remember every trespass or sin has two components; that is temptation and acceptance of the temptation.

Therefore the deceiver or the thief (Satan) is more at fault than us, because he has knowledge and understands the spirit world better. It is best for us to just forgive and better bless and love your enemies as God has commanded us.

Matthew 5:39 *But I say unto you. That you resist not evil: but whosoever shall smite you on the right cheek, turn to him the other also.* Do not fight back, take the high road, and just walk away.

In forgiveness you release the brother from sin but not the evil one. Trust in the promise of God that He will repay, what was stolen. When God repays, it is always a double portion. When we forgive, we also store our treasure in Heaven; for it is the will of God for us to forgive those who trespass against us. **Matthew 6:12**

Rom 12:20 *Therefore, if your enemy hunger, feed him, if he thirst, give him drink: for in doing you shall heap coals of fire on his head.* By showing kindness to an enemy, we are diverting judgment, and show mercy; which Christ has demonstrated to us. We become more and more Christ like in character.

Rom 12:21 *Be not overcome of evil, but overcome evil with good.* The old saying "Eye for an eye and tooth for a tooth", only breeds more evil and hate.

We accomplish nothing. So as **Members of the Body of Christ,** we must depart from this situation. By showing mercy to others, we also receive mercy from God. At the same time we also store our treasures in Heaven, as Christ has commanded us. And best of all, we bear fruit.

Exhortation:

1Tim 2:1 *I exhort therefore that, first of all, supplications* (ask for blessings of personal needs), *prayers* (for petitions), *intercessions* (for praying for others who may not know God Our Savior), *and of giving thanks, be made for all men;* When praying for others, please, mention the name of the person. Thereby your prayers are effective. The person you want blessed will be blessed. Why did Jesus call the name of Lazarus? If the name Lazarus was not mentioned, all the dead at that time might all get up.

1 Tim. 2:2 *For kings, and for all who are in authority; that we may lead a quiet and peaceable life in all godliness and honesty.* A government whose leaders are with moral integrity: and are without corruption and greed for power, but of pure heart and of service to its citizens that it promised to serve. Happy are they; for in Heaven they shall occupy a higher seat.

1 Timothy 2:3 *For this is good in the Sight of God our Saviour.* What is good in God's eyes, is good for all mankind, and for men in authority are servants of God and of his fellow men, and that is a privilege to be called to serve.

What is Love?

Matthew 5:44 *But I say unto you, Love your enemies, bless them who curse you, do good to them who hate you, and pray for them which despitefully use you, and persecute you.*

Obeying this commandment satisfies God's second law, "Love thy neighbor as you Love yourself". Actually this is one of the requisite for becoming a **Member of the Body of Christ.**

I have met a lot of people who says, that this is the hardest commandment to obey. They said, "I cannot imagine loving someone who has inflicted me with so much hurt". At first when I heard this, I have nothing to say. But now, I can't agree with them and I realized that this verse is still not fully understood even by those who have professed that accepted Christ as their Lord and Savior. Apparently, they still don't know the consequences of not loving our enemies. It becomes a stumbling block and if we can't forgive and love those who have hurt us, then we are not **Members of the Body of Christ.** Because there is still hate in our hearts.

Hate cannot reign in the **Kingdom of God**. Let us check what the Lord's Prayer say "Forgive our debts as we forgive our debtors". Definitely, the Gospel of Love must be preached with zest and urgency, so that no one will be left behind, when Rupture of the Church takes place very soon.

Do Not Swear: Words are Significant: There is a saying: Be careful of what you wish for. Because errant words, always comes back to haunt you.

Matthew 5:33 *Again, you have heard that it has been said by them of the old time. You shall not foreswear yourself, but shall perform unto the Lord your oaths.*

Matthew 5:34 *But I say unto you, Swear not at all, neither by Heaven; for it is the God's Throne.*

Matthew 5:35 *Nor by the Earth; for it is my footstool, neither by Jerusalem; for it is the city of the great King.*

Matthew 5:37 *But your communication be, Yes, yes; No, no, for whatsoever is more than these comes of evil.*

In the above verses, as **Members of the Body of Christ,** we are instructed by Christ how to properly conduct ourselves in our conversation with one another. There cannot be any deception in our conversations with others. The members are not allowed to do evil works in the name of Jesus, for it is using the name of God in vain. For the act of deception is of the devil and it has no place in the Kingdom of God. The following virtue applies: truthfulness, honesty, kindness, and integrity. Story telling a lie, and double talk are not allowed.

Matt. 16:18 *And I say also unto you, that you are Peter, and upon this rock I will build my Church; and the gates of Hell shall not prevail against it.*

Jesus Christ said to Peter/Simon: On this Rock (symbolizes Earth or Father God) I will build my Church. Become a member of His Church. Anything is possible.

Matt. 116:19 *And I will give unto you the keys of the Kingdom of Heaven: and whatsoever you shall bind on earth shall be bound in Heaven: and whatsoever you shall loose on earth shall be loosed in Heaven.* As a **Member of the Body of Christ,** we are authorized by Jesus to bind and rebuke evil in His Name.

Suggestion:

I urge the President of the USA to declare publicly to cast out evil spirits out of this country to remove the many stumbling blocks that is preventing the country to becoming a greater nation, a nation under God. Every Head of State, governors or head of a City has that authority. The Church, Bishops and Pastors must also do likewise.

Proof: Pres. Ronald Reagan broke down the USSR by declaring that it is an Evil Empire. In 1990 the Berlin wall fell down. Very few Americans give him credit.

In Nov. 2013, Albay and Sorsogon, Philippines were spared from the destruction of typhoon Yolanda when the Governor asked the people to pray. Miracles can happen. Proof that God listens and answers prayers.

CHAPTER 25

Judgment of God

The Judgment on the False Prophets of Babylon:

Jeremiah 29:21 *Thus says the Lord of Host, the God of Israel, of Ahab the son of Kolaiah, and of Zedekiah the son of Masseiah, which prophesy a lie unto you in my name; Behold, I will deliver them into the hand of Nebuchadnezzar king of Babylon, and he shall kill them before your eyes.* Do not blaspheme God for we will be punished.

Jeremiah 29:23 *Because they have committed villany in Israel, and have committed adultery with their neighbors' wives, and have spoken lying words in My Name, which I have not commanded them; even I know, and am a witness says the Lord.* God is all knowing.

Why Bad Things Happens to Good People?

People all around the world are always asking this question all the time. We hear the complaints especially; during aftermath of calamities like the earthquake of Haiti, like the huge tsunami in Indonesia and recently, typhoons like Yolanda in the Philippines. We witness tremendous sufferings of people. Truly these events are heart breaking. And our sympathy goes to all who suffered the most.

Likewise, even local families have experienced harrowing events in their lives that are very brutal and hard to comprehend. What they will always ask is that, why would God, **if He is a good God, allow bad things happen to good people?** I believe the religious community has not done a good job of explaining. Why does it happen? Until now many people are clueless.

First of all, people must know that being a good person based on this world's standards does not guarantee salvation. Only the saving grace and mercy of God through Jesus Christ guarantees salvation.

As of this writing, more and more bad events are happening at the highest frequency in the history of this world. So many people are saying that the End Time of the Church Age is at hand. Ok. Therefore, it is about time that a comprehensive answer must be brought out and be understood.

To Stop Bad things from Happening; The Biblical Answer: **Romans 8:28-39. We must become More than Conquerors:** The following verses will tell us how.

Rom. 8:28 *And we know that all things work together for good to them who love God, to them who are called according to His purpose.* These are the two conditions: 1) to them who love God, are **Members of the Body of Christ**, 2) According to His purpose – God's purpose must prevail, not ours.

Rom. 8:29 *For whom He (God) did foreknow, He also did predestinate to be conformed to the image of His Son, that He (Jesus) might be the Firstborn among many brethren.* God the Father, predestinate Jesus as the Firstfruit, so that all who believes in Him will be conformed to Christ's image.

Rom. 8:30 *Moreover whom He (God) did predestinate, them He also called: and whom He called, them He also justified: and whom He justified; them He also glorified.*

Happy are those whom He called, because with out God's calling we will not come into the knowledge of Christ and be able to respond faithfully to the call. And once this condition is satisfied, we will also be justified and glorified.

Rom 8:31 *What shall we then say to these things? If God be for us, who can be against us?*

Now to explain further, if we are not in Christ and Christ is not in us, or we are not **Members of the Body of Christ,** or we are not in the **Kingdom of God;** in essence we are outsiders, outside of the protection of God and we are free games for the emissaries of the destroyer or Satan. These emissaries are all over this Earth, they know if you are a free game or not.

Therefore, don't give them a chance to touch, to tempt or opportunity to do their evil deeds on you. It is never enough to be just good, for all of us need the armor of God. Wear them all the time. We need to be a **Member of the Body of Christ.**

Cover yourself with prayers for safety, speak the words to tell your holy angels to provide protection every day and every time you leave home.

Accidents don't just happen, I believe 90% of the time there is an evil one behind it, and 10% are due to human negligence. We take things for granted, even if we know that something is wrong or not right in our tools that we use, or in our environment. Therefore, the **man of the house** must be watchful of little things that can go wrong. **Don't give the evil one, a chance to destroy your life and the lives of your loved ones.** Stay in Christ Jesus all the time and never let go, for only in Him you find keep.

When bad things happens in our lives, we feel that God allows it to happen, but in reality, the Holy Spirit has already given us warnings. Most of the time we are too busy to give credit to the good works of God and we fail to discern God's voice. Let us not blame God.

It is man's failure to listen and act on the counsel of the Holy Spirit that prompts God to allow it to happen. I believe in many cases also, it becomes God's way of waking us, because we do not listen. But we are not supposed to suffer. God does not want us to suffer in misery. Therefore we must be conscientious in all the things we do.

Watch the daily evening news. Most of the time you will see criminal acts like murder, burglary, suicide bombing and terrorism by Islamic groups, kidnapping, rape and all sorts of crimes are committed left and right by seemingly very nice people. Did you ever wonder why all these grotesque events are happening? All of them are inspired by evil. Committed by people who are possessed by demonic spirits. These crimes are the result of people whose hearts and minds are too far away from the Saving Grace of our Lord Jesus Christ. They knew no God.

Another reason for this is the removal of prayer in Public School Systems in the USA and in other Christian countries, but it is worse in Islamic countries where terrorism, and hate for Jews and Christians is the thought of the day.

Rom. 8:35 *Who shall separate us from the Love of Christ? Shall tribulation, or distress, or persecution, or nakedness, or peril, or sword?* No one can, if we will not allow the evil one to deceive us.

Rom. 8:36 *As it is written, For your sake we are killed all day long; we are accounted as sheep for the slaughter.*

Rom.8:37 *Nay, in all these things we are more than conquerors, through Him Who loved us.*

Rom. 8:38 *For I am persuaded, that neither death, nor life, nor Angels, nor principalities, nor powers, nor things present, nor things to come.*

Rom. 8:39 *Nor height, nor depth, nor any other creature, shall be able to separate us from the Love of God, which is in Christ Jesus our Lord.* With verses 35-39; We are assured by God, that no one can do bad things to us, if we are with Christ. Bad things happen only if we are separated from our Lord Jesus, meaning we are not **Members of the Body of Christ.** Sometimes we forget our first love Jesus Christ because of the cares of this world and we are cut off from the Vine.

God's Mercy:

Deuteronomy 8:3 *And He humbled you, and suffered you to hunger, and fed you with manna, which you knew not, neither did your fathers know, that He might make you know that man does not live by bread only, but by every word that proceeds out of the Mouth of the Lord does man live.* We must know where our blessings are coming from.

CHAPTER 26

Second Coming of Jesus Christ

Get Ready:

1 Thess. 3:11 *Now God Himself and Our Father, and Our Lord Jesus Christ, direct our way unto you.*

1 Thess. 3:12 *And the Lord make you to increase and abound in love one toward another, and toward all men, even as we do toward you.*

1 Thess. 3:13 *To the end He may stablish your hearts unblameable in Holiness before God, even our Father, at the coming of our Lord Jesus Christ with all His Saints.*

Day of the Lord:

2 Peter 3:10 *But the Day of he Lord will come as a thief in the night; in the which the Heavens shall pass away with a great noise, and the elements shall be melt with fervent heat, the Earth also and the works that are therein shall be burned up.*

2 Peter 3:11 *Seeing then that all theses shall be dissolved, what manner of persons ought ye to be in all Holy conversation and Godliness.*

2 Peter 3:12 *Looking for and hasting unto the Coming of the Day of God, wherein the Heavens being on fire shall be dissolved, and the elements shall be melt with fervent heat?*

2 Peter 3:13 *Nevertheless we, according to His Promise, look for a new Heavens and a new Earth, wherein dwells Righteousness.*

Signs of the End Times:

Luke 21:8 *And He said, Take heed that you be not deceived; for many shall come in my Name, saying, I am Christ; and the time draws near; go ye not therefore after them.*

We are warned not to be deceived again, so we must be very careful in following anyone. Christ is telling us to validate anyone who claims to be Him. We must know His Words, the Gospel of Christ; the words contained in the Holy Bible. If we know that we are **Members of the body of Christ**, we must not worry, for we are in good hands.

Luke 21:9 *But when you shall hear of wars and commotions, be not terrified: for these things must first come to pass; but the end is not by and by.*

Luke 21:10 *Then said He unto them, Nation shall rise against nations, and kingdom against kingdom;*

Luke 21:11 *And great earthquakes shall be in divers places, and famines, and pestilences, and fearful sights and great signs shall there be from Heaven.* We are being warned that these days will come no matter what man does. It is time to secure our place in the Body of Christ where we will be protected from all these tribulations.

The Second Advent of Christ

Revelation 19:11 *And I saw Heaven opened, and behold a white horse; and He Who sat upon him was called Faithful and True, and in Righteousness He does Judge and make war.* To see a more complete of the revelation of Christ Second Coming, read Rev. 19:12-15

Rev. 19:16 *And He has on His vesture and on His thigh a name written, KING OF KINGS, AND LORD OF LORDS.*

We have to study End Time Prophecies.

Notes:

Take heed: Our Father in Heaven might be unseen, but He is a big part of our daily lives.

CHAPTER 27

The Stumbling Blocks

The following social issues are pulling us down. It is putting our spiritual welfare in a no win situation. We must not worry too much about the health of our flesh. Eventually we have to shed it for it is a corrupted body, impregnated with the sin nature of Satan. Certainly we all die in this flesh. But we must not die in the Spirit, for we have our advocate to our Father in Christ Jesus. We must cast away Satan so that we remove these Stumbling Blocks.

1) Suicide, What Terrible Thing to Do

Although God has given man the privilege of Free Will, it does not mean God approves that man shall oppose Him. We must realize that man is the apple of God's eyes.

Judas Iscariot repented when he realized, he made a horrible mistake by being a traitor to his master Jesus Christ. But he listened to the voice of Satan blaming him and so he hanged himself. One of his biggest lie. I can say without a doubt in my mind, that he (Judas) is spiritually dead. Why? Jesus has declared that it is better for Judas Iscariot not to have been born. That there is no chance: for the salvation of his spirit. And these apply to all: who have committed suicide or has taken their own life by any means. Only our Creator God can take our Life. No other has that right. Please, please my brothers and sisters, take heed, because in **killing your own body, you are killing your spirit. For sure your spirit will go to Hell. Please choose Paradise.**

Once you murdered your own body, **your spirit and soul are with Satan,** there is no way you can have the privilege of Salvation from Hell or Lake of Fire, 'cause Jesus did not dwell in you, and you in Him.

Only the in-dwelling of Christ in our hearts can guarantee Salvation. Christ had paid the ransom for our sins at the Cross. Why waste this privilege? When God had promised, those who believe in His Son shall not perish but will gain everlasting life, so much wonderful things.

I also believe that you will not be even part of the Great White Throne Judgment. You already did exact judgment on yourself. It is finished. There is nothing to judge in you. How sad is that.

Also, please don't make jokes or pranks about suicide issue, because the thief, the killer, the deceiver and the destroyer of our God given Life; are also listening all the time. Be very careful of what words you say. Remember the saying: Be careful of what you wish for. For something bad might happen. It is true. I am not kidding. You don't want to believe me?

Try it, just be ready for the consequences. Warning: you might not be up to the challenge. Remember, you are not, protected by God in these situations.

*(A **personal story**: My barber, a gay guy in his mid thirties has a boyfriend in his mid twenties. He said that his boyfriend text him one night, that he is depressed and is thinking of killing himself, and my barber's response was jokingly, and he text back, "Go Ahead, do what you want to do". About 3 days later, the youngster is dead.)*

The young man's soul and spirit is surely not going to heaven and will not spend his spirit life with our Lord Jesus and our Father. He will be spending it in Hell. Therefore it is not worth it to play Russian Roulette with your spirit.

Do not oppose God. Do not hate God. Opposing and hating God, your creator, is the same as committing Suicide. You are killing yourself. **See Prov. 8:36** *But he who sins against me wrongs his own soul, all they who hate me love death.*

Remember; God is the owner of our spirit because God created us first in the spirit and soul (male and female). And the soul (our feelings like love, hate, anger or dismay, and our 5 senses) connects us to our flesh and bones. Then Jesus molded man in dust in His form, then breath on his nostrils. And man (Adam) was a living soul. See **Gen. 2:7** *And the Lord God formed man of the dust of the ground, and breathed into his nostrils the breath of life, and man became a living soul.*

Therefore, don't ever believe anyone or anybody saying that when you are dead in your flesh that all your problems in this

243

earth are no more. And worse, some people will tell you that you will be in a better place. How can we be in a better place if we are not dwelling in Christ or we are not Member of the Body of Christ? **Again, another big lie, by the destroyer and accuser.**

If Robin Williams committed suicide, the Scriptures says it is better he has not been born, similar to Judas Iscariot's fate. Therefore he is not in a better place. The best place is to be in Paradise.

Think more than a million times.

Your real tribulations and sufferings are just beginning, and are eternal. Suffering beyond compare. Hell is real. Imagine you will be in the Lake of fire? Why gamble on the destiny of your spirit and soul, where you can secure it now to belong to the Body of Christ who is in Paradise.

2) On Gay and Lesbian Issue

On my trips abroad, for my haircut and manicure services, I choose those beauty parlors owned and operated by gays. I love their services. I like and appreciate their excellent work. They are very good at it. And I have great respect for them as humans. They are hard working people. It does not bother me, however they act, it is fun and hilarious. And their jokes are really funny and I treat them the way I want to be treated; of course, with respect. I don't care what people do behind closed doors.

Many times I asked them (gay guys) what makes them act like girls. They have one answer: Their emotions and feelings are that they are complete girls or women, and that is the main reason they seek men. And the lesbians feel they are macho man. And they seek women. Their feelings are real and they are not made up for the sake of any agenda. I truly understand the situation and have sympathy on their predicament. It is not easy.

It does not bother me if the government (state) gives them the right to be certified and recognized as a couple joined together. I cannot be very legalistic on this issue. Because of man's free will: Who am I to judge? I will leave the judgment to God. But I have to remind my fellow citizens of this world, that they cannot use the word **marriage** to describe their union because I believe God will not get involve in their agreement. God will not bend His ways to fit man's desire. As for me I will respect the desire of the gay groups, but I will also ask them to respect my faith and that they will not tamper with my belief and keep the sanctity of word **"marriage"**, solely a union between a man and a woman. Once there is an agreement between man and woman to love each other, I know God is involved as the Heavens rejoice when a man takes a wife.

It is my prayer that the gay groups must just use other terms to describe their union, to eliminate any animosity and disagreement. They are potentially still my brothers and sisters in the spirit. **So I have to warn you:**

He is a just and righteous God, we can turn to Him in times of trouble. So please make that call.

I know God does not approve of homosexuality. Whatever the gay groups do, to seek approval of their union, it may have acceptance here on Earth, but it will never be acceptable to God in Heaven.

245

What good is it then to work hard for nothing? He did not create Adam and Adam. Adam and Adam cannot bear the fruit of the womb and it's not pleasing in God's eyes. He created Adam and Eve and performed their marriage. God has already provided us the avenue to get out sin thru faith in Christ.

Gen. 1:28 God said unto them: *Be fruitful, and multiply, and replenish the Earth and subdue it:* . . . Adam and Adam cannot fulfill this command. Simply it is not acceptable to Him that we cannot pro-create, the very purpose we are created. I don't believe God will ever change, because He is the same yesterday, today and tomorrow. That is His nature. Man does not have the power to change that. We are the creation not the Creator. And we cannot boast. If we try it our way, we are opposing Him. Opposing God is sin. Therefore, we will be cast out of His presence. That only means one thing. We are dead. There is nothing to gain and actually a lot of loss to disobey. **Obeying God is the only way.** Learn to love God.

Just like in man he created a car. He can do anything to the car. But the car can't do anything to him. The car is only a creation. Powerless.

Think of it this way. In an analogy: As a car where do you want to be: **in a showroom or in a junkyard?** The answer is a no brainer. Just obey what God says. There is absolutely no point in being contentious and wrestling with God. Jacob wrestled with God, but in the end he won't let go until God blesses him.

But when it comes to state of **SPIRITUAL WELLNESS;** that is where I have to seek for answers in the spiritual realm, because even in the natural world, their circumstances does not fit the Creation model of the True God I know. For sure, it is not their fault. I will not put any blame on them because the free will factor of the individual was never involved.

In my search for answers, I will not consider their abnormality as a medical problem. Their flesh and blood, in my view functions perfectly. The problem is in the soul and spirit. It was corrupted. That is where the malady occurred. Spiritual abnormality: every one has this. I understand, it will be very difficult for us; people to qualify, or quantify the things in the spiritual realm, because supernatural things are not easily understood. Our 5 senses cannot comprehend these things. It does not respond to. That's why we need to understand the written Word of God as our guide to understand the spiritual realm.

All mankind has spiritual malady or affliction; therefore the problem of gays and lesbian is not an isolated case that it needs different remedy. That it requires any especial treatment or any law to enhance or protect them. All they need is respect and understanding of their situation. Of course no one has the right to mock or bully anybody just because he or she looks or acts differently and weird.

All of mankind, are on the same boat (Noah built only one boat), for the population of one Rock (the third rock from the sun), we are all sinners by genealogy. All must come unto repentance to have Hope.

The Bible says all, no exceptions. Read Matthew 3:2.

The Only Solution is Jesus Christ.

We must **trust** in Him. If He can transform the water into a very excellent wine, raise Lazarus from the dead and be alive again, make Sarah, the wife of Abraham fertile, heal the lepers and make the blind see. He can also do the same for all of us. He can transform us to be Spiritually alive and be normal physically. There is nothing impossible with God. All it takes is repentance and faith. **It is a matter of choice**.

I firmly believe families with sons and daughters that are either gay or lesbian did not have the protection of the Holy Spirit when they were conceived. The evil one tampered these children during conception. (Remember the story of Sodom and Gomorrah, why God destroyed it? The same thing is happening now. The destroyer is tampering the unborn children at a very high rate and advising those that are inflicted to go for equality). Worse.

For lack of knowledge and wisdom, their parents did not ask or pray for protection from the evil one **who comes to steal, kill and destroy.** The husband is mostly to blame, for failure to act as High Priest of the house. It is the duty of the husband to teach and to lead the family to prayer. Joshua said: **As for me, and my household, we will serve the Lord.**

In the absence of God in the family, the sad result is that our children suffered from other spiritual affliction aside from sin. Our lack of godly behavior translated into abnormality of emotions in the children. Therefore it is important that a Spiritual Marriage between man and wife performed by Christ as our High Priest occurs. It becomes a sanctified union. Now this family becomes a **Member of the Body of Christ**, wherein we obtain blessings to bear good fruit and protection from the destroyer and accuser. It is very comforting to know that our family is protected from spiritual affliction. Our life in the flesh and bones are not completely protected from mortal sickness. We have to die from this corrupt flesh in order to be sanctified.

I understand nobody wants to be homosexual. So what are we doing? At present we are re-inventing the wheel with laws to allow same sex union. Another sad thing, we feel it is the right answer to the problem. But actually it is not the solution.

Here is the sad truth. Love hurts. Whatever we do to legalize the issue, the problem will not go away. God will never recognize same sex union because it is an opposition to God's ways and if we continue our worldly ways we remain apart from Him. So what is the point in opposing God? Nothing. The Bible says: **Mark 8:36** *For what shall it profit a man, if he shall gain the whole world, and will lose his soul?* Big Fat Nothing. Our soul is worth more than the whole world to our God.

Don't worry, the cure or remedy is also spiritual. Again, **Christ is only the solution.** He can do everything and nothing is impossible with God. Our Father is the Most High God. Therefore, it is important that we must be grafted in the True Vine all the time. **John 15:1**. Repent and accept Christ and be a **Member of the Body of Christ. Being an insider we are protected 24/7/366.** Our blessings abounds. Once an insider, you will know it is not hard to follow Jesus. It is very easy. Opposition or rebellion is what makes it hard.

I have 3 family friends wherein the husband could have opted to practice homosexuality. Instead they got married and had a wife and children and lived a normal life. The husbands still talk and act like gay men. My question: if these 3 men can escape homosexual lifestyle, how come so many cannot do it? Is it willfully or knowingly to oppose God? I pray not. I believe my 3 friends feared God, and they know the consequences of rebellion to God. We have to obey for our own good.

To all homosexuals, here is your warning: Because of free will: Do what you have to do. But remember the most important thing is to save your soul. Forget about equality, legal rights, and acquiring wealth through corruption for these things don't please and don't glorify God. He will not recognizes same sex union for it does not profit Him.

3) Abortion: an Abomination in God's Eyes

I do not subscribe to the belief that man can do anything to his body is because he owns it. That he or she has the privilege to abort a child after conception has occurred in the womb. Therefore he or she has no accountability, responsibility and cannot be held liable for any consequence by Mortal Law (State) as well as Spiritual Law (God's). Without a doubt, this is another Satan's (the killer) big lie, and man has bought into it, big time. **Think again if you plan to have Abortion.**

Again, Adam and Eve in the Garden of Eden re-visited. I cannot believe men are still so foolish, even in this age of high technology, with all this new discoveries and inventions, we think we are wiser now. But no, man has not learned his lessons well.

In the Mortal Law, Roe vs. Wade edict by the US Supreme Court allowed abortion to happen in America. It gives the woman the right to abort pregnancy, because they claim, the woman owns her body and the fetus, or even a seven month old baby in the womb is not a person yet. It resulted in the killing of innocent lives.

At the moment, abortion is going on in clinics around the nation; and these acts are being championed and perpetrated by Planned Parenthood, Inc, a legal business entity.

It could be up to millions of babies slaughtered every year. What a shame to be in the business of killing babies and making money to feed your family at the expense of innocent babies who cannot defend themselves. I wonder what kind of conscience does these people have? On top of it, subsidized by the government. I cringed at this thought. Truth is they don't own their bodies.

I believe the killer spirit is very happy about this. No wonder our country is suffering so much this past decade. Too many Americans are out work and pan handling in the corner of the streets of America. God's vengeance is now apparent.

And new jobs reported are mostly low paying jobs. Where is the America I used to know?

This type of sin will not go unpunished by God. God's blessing to America has come in trickles lately. Does our government officials, takes notice of the trend? That we are in decay? I pray they will. America is still an anointed country. We used to typify a land with flowing milk and honey; a land of great abundance. But now, it is diminishing at a pace that we cannot deny it. **I**

will pray that my country can find its way back to God, very soon. ASAP.

But the Holy Bible says it is murder, therefore it is a sin against God. Where, life of man and woman on earth starts at conception in the womb of a mother.

Therefore, we don't have the right to take life. God is the sole owner of our body, and He created us in spirit first and then in flesh, blood and bones. See **Gen. 1:27, Gen. 2:7**! God has the final judgment to take our breath away. When? It is God's call, and not yours and mine.

Let us make these things clear, the Spirit in man! Gen. 1:27 *So God created man in His own image, in the image of God created He him; male and female created He them.* v. 26 say . . . *after Our Likeness.* Therefore every human being, that lived this Earth started with a male or female spirit first, and all of those that will be born in the future.

Then in **Gen 2:7** God gave flesh and bones to the male spirit, and now Adam is a living soul. Then Eve was created from the left rib of Adam and was given a body with a female spirit. In all of God's creation only humans are accorded with a spirit just like God's spirit. In His image and likeness. So you and I are begotten with a spirit. This we cannot deny, our sense of feeling validates the presence of spiritual component in us, especially when we start to seek God. Trust me on this.

We must understand this truth: Man's first life is in the spirit and his second life is in the flesh, blood and bones. If Adam ate the fruit of the Tree of Life, Man's two state of being would have been reconciled long time ago in the Garden of Eden and living happily ever after with his Creator. But since he ate the fruit of the tree with evil instead, that is the reason why man life is still in this state of quagmire. We must take heart and let us not be troubled, for Christ is ready come back soon to finally, completely and ultimately claim us who are Members of the Body of Christ from the community of evil spirits. When Christ and us binds Satan and send him to the bottomless pit after the great battle, also going with him all his emissaries. Furthermore, I believe including the human souls who allowed themselves to be deceived by the evil lie. A lesson learned here, never allow to be deceived. Trust the Word of God to be true, because it is true.

So, Adam and Eve were not begotten, they were created. The next generations of humans are all begotten. Eve was created to become the vehicle for man's regeneration process. God commanded us; go and multiply.

At conception, God will assign a spirit either male or female. The type of spirit male or female will determine the gender of the baby. The spirit commands the outcome, not the flesh. The Bible does not mention of homosexual spirits. I have not read anything that points to it. Even angels mentioned are all male. The Bible does not mention of female angels, either holy or fallen.

Now to answer the question: **Why are homosexuals born into the world?**

My answer to the reader: Go and connect the dots. I have given the scenario from previous section.

Before conception of the baby, a living spirit is already at stake. Now, after conception, the spirit is looking forward for a life on Earth, to showcase his God given gifts, talents and potential to be great and to glorify his maker.

And now comes the destroyer and whispered to the mother, it's not worth keeping the baby for various reasons, go to Planned Parenthood. Abort! Abort! Abort! Suddenly the fetus is killed. How would you feel if it's your life being aborted?

This fetus will be one of our brother or sister one day. How about if this fetus can only shout, STOP killing me! Are we willing to hear and heed? Very, very sad, indeed that it is happening in this USA. We are supposed to be highly educated, and yet we are acting moronic.

And just because abortion was legalized; by the bums of the US Supreme Court, it does not mean it is the right thing to do. **Look up young man, look up! Think.** We have to think about the consequences for the spirit not just our welfare here on Earth but also those who are in the spirit world. Every body deserves a chance to live a full and meaningful life. God's command is Love one another. Why can't we do just that? It is simple enough. Why listen to the accuser?

This is the reason why Life is sacred to God and it should be the same for all of us too. God's command is; Thou shall not murder. Our God is an equal opportunity God, He gives us a level playing field. Our God is a capitalist. He is a rich God with unlimited wealth to give to everyone of us. Our God is not a God of poverty and misery. It is man who has the problem.

We will not starve if we only find our way (Jesus) back to Him (to become a **Member of the Body of Christ,** this position gives us all we ask of our Father). He wants all His human creation to have the chance to achieve all their potential and to glorify Him. Our Father in Heaven is a **Capitalist.**

If we stop aborting our babies, and we even fill this Earth with humans to the brim and let these babies reach their full potential, is not our concern. I know God will be happy and the whole Heaven rejoice, because we bear fruit. It is God's problem to feed us all. We only have to open our hearts to receive them.

The problem is not ours. If He (Jesus) can multiply 5 loaves of bread and 2 fishes to feed 5 to 25 thousands of people and still have left over's? It is a great miracle. I expect the same thing to happen, when this world is full of people.

God's command is go and multiply, He did not say **stop multiplying at,** before I told you so.

How we come unto this Earth:

Jeremiah 1:5 *Before I formed you in the belly I knew you and before you came forth out of the womb I sanctified you, and I ordained you a Prophet unto the nations.*

Two versions of exposition of the verse Jeremiah 1:5 and I quote.

"(From the Expositor's Study Bible by Jimmy Swaggart: In this, one can easily see the Doctrine of Predestination. But only that the Lord through foreknowledge "knew", what kind of man Jeremiah would be, and not that Jeremiah had been denied the power of choice and had been forced by God into a certain course of action.

"I sanctified you" refers to the call of Jeremiah, that he had been set apart for the particular use.

"I ordained you a Prophet unto the nations" means appointed. His message would involve not only Israel, but also those nations, which had to do with Israel.)"

Jeremiah 1:5 is a proof that life exist before and after conception and all its inalienable rights comes along with it.

It also tells us that God "knew" us before our conception into the womb (an act of God) because He is the Creator of our spirit. We are alive in the spirit first, **Gen. 1:26-27.** Life already exists. Therefore no one has the right to abort our predestined existence on Earth except God.

Everyone should be given a chance to reach, achieve and enjoy our God given potential. This is also an illustration that God is in control of everything in this universe. Furthermore, this verse validates Genesis, Chapter 1.

At conception the fetus is already a person. That is starting life of a human being. But life in the spirit of that person has started and has been alive a long time. Only God knows how long, before a match was made. For it takes 9 months for the baby, to develop all its organs and its body to survive life on earth. Therefore, it takes 9 months to convert spirit life to carnal life. In the Roman Catholic belief, it also takes 9 days/nights of prayer for the dead, to convert the carnal life back to spirit life. The spirit life is eternal. Whether it will be spent in Heaven or in Hell.

And because of this knowledge, I recommend that: Roe vs. Wade must be overturned by Congress and by the citizens of America. Abortion is: the legalized killing of American people.

It is another tool of our enemy. Let us not be deceived again, and again and again.

The Supreme Court Justices should have considered the existence of life before and after conception. Were they blinded by evil?

What happened to their oath by placing their hands on the Bible? **Do they believe that human rights are greater than the Will of God, our Creator?**

If it is, then the People of USA must be given by the Constitution more power than any branch of government, so the people can remove radical Justices from the bench.

A Constitutional Amendment must be in the works.

My prayer to our Father in Heaven: **that the carnage of innocent unborn babies will STOP now.**

I believe abortion is one the devil's tool in opposing God and delaying the Second Advent of Christ.

Our Task: Finding a Real Solution

To our society: let us stop the culture of chastising unmarried women when they get pregnant; before marriage. Let us remove the stigma associated out of unwanted pregnancy. Remember we are living in an unholy world and it is not perfect. The Tree of Knowledge of Good and Evil is still with us and temptation still abounds. Man is still falling for the lie of Evil over and over again and the Scriptures say we have to love all and forgive all who trespass against us.

If a woman gets pregnant: married or not, let us rejoice and welcome the baby. Even for teenage pregnancy. God says love one another.

If the baby is in some way has genetic problems; like down syndrome and was detected by medical procedure, while in the womb, let us pray that the baby will be fine when born. I urge the government, business and religious groups to set up a fund to take care of these babies.

Orphanages and other similar institutions are fine, but give the mother priority to take care. If the mother has a change of mind after years of absence from the child and want to have her child, let her with no questions asked.

Selective abortion cannot be allowed either. It can only be possible if the mother's life is threatened. Other than this, there will be no more exception.

Let us disallow Planned Parenthood and all other abortion clinics in doing business around the nation. Close down all.

Although I consent not to chastise unwanted pregnancy, it does not mean, I do not want to adhere to normal and proper order of doing things, like having a family. It is an act of love to fellow man. Our God is a God of Order. But the act of murdering innocent unborn babies is the worst thing to do. I subscribe to giving leeway for mistakes, for we are all sinners. None of us is perfect. But for this issue of abortion, I will not just sit down and watch.

I know I have offended pro-choice supporters. But I am not going to apologize, because I know I am doing the right thing and ordained to oppose evil. Besides I do not represent any status quo or agenda based organizations. My opposition is not for my own benefit. As a citizen of this world, it is my duty to protect, and serve the weak and the powerless. Love hurts.

I represent the Word of God.

Another proof that a living spirit is needed for the conception of human beings. In the case of the Virgin Birth of Jesus Christ: We are told that Virgin Mary was given notice by the Archangel Gabriel that she will overshadowed by the Spirit of God, and she will conceive a baby boy, and they will name Him Jesus.

Therefore, for every conception to happen there is a living spirit involved in the procreation of life. Again, no one has the right to take life, except God. Let us pray to cast out evil every day, that we not be tempted and be deceived by Satan again to oppose God; especially the horrible sin of murder: Abortion.

What the Gosnell Trial has Revealed: Featured in: The Week Magazine, April 26, 2013 Issue. Excerpts: And I quote;

"Haven't heard about these sickening accusations? It's not your fault," said Kirsten Powers in USA Today. Since the murder trial of Philadelphia abortion doctor Kermit Gosnell began last month, the mainstream media has almost entirely ignored a "case that should be on every news show and front page" Gosnell, who is charged with killing seven infants born alive and a woman who died during a botched procedure, operated a charnel house where abortions were routinely carried out past Pennsylvania's 24 week limit."

Of course Liberal Main Stream Media will not give much deserved coverage of this case. They will not accept guilt, and will hide from the issue, hoping the pro-life sector of our society will soon forget. I thank God for revisiting and keeping the issue alive in one of the TV Networks after over a year of Gosnell conviction of this heinous crime.

It is a big slap on the faces of the main supporters of abortion and pro-choice agenda. It would be a shame on them. They do not serve the Public's interest and serve only their evil twisted agenda. Another group of people: who are badly deceived by the destroyer of human life.

In this case, God is telling us to STOP abortion. He is asking: **Why are you persecuting Me?**

I further quote *"Liberal Media outlets would have given this wall-to-wall, sensational coverage" if Gosnell had killed dogs" said Erick Ericson in RedState.com. But since he only murdered babies, they largely buried their heads, fearing it would expose the true horror of legalized abortion."* Legalized Murder of unborn babies. This sin carries very high punishment. For sure God will exact vengeance, as it is written. God will not forget.

Abortion is murder, period.

Our Responsibilities

A very, very grave sin, the bad consequences are ultra high, not only to the perpetrators, but more to the whole nation, for the state is the one who instituted the legalization. The mechanism for the murder was being carried out by corporate clinics and corporations, they are like individuals created by the state.

Unlike homosexuality and suicide is a choice against yourself and God. And you know the consequences. Abortion issue is another. Clearly, abortion is a sin against your future brothers and sisters, and of course against God.

Abortion is something, where we cannot exercise our own individual free will. We cannot encroach on the rights of others. The individual rights of the unborn baby must be respected and protected, as well as our responsibility to feed and clothe them, shelter and to teach them the Word of God. So they will grow in the knowledge and wisdom that there is a one True and Good God. "Teach them diligently, **Deut. 6:7**". To make these children: good citizens of this world. Actually this is all the wisdom we need.

As adult and responsible citizens of the world, we have the obligation; to protect the weak, the innocent and the powerless, such are these unborn babies.

And what are we doing? Killing them instead for what gain? Now their blood is on us.

God will not allow us to trample on the lives of these innocent unborn individuals forever. They maybe small and seems insignificant but there is life in them. I don't want to see God's wrath on USA, but I know it is forthcoming as the country struggles with its economy, morality as crime is rising and with its diminishing superpower status.

Example: China and Russia are bullies of their weaker neighbors now. USA can only watch. Proof that maybe we are war weary? Or our President is a wimp. Or God's punishment for America's sins is already taking place. Can't you see 30 years later after Roe vs. Wade? God's vengeance is upon us.

It is not the same America I have known since I immigrated to this great country 30 years ago.

So my advice: **America open up your eyes. Look up, young man, look up. Repent! Repeal Roe vs. Wade.** Repeal the new Health Care Law. Allow prayers back in Public Schools. These Laws has taken away valuable rights of the people and they are unconstitutional. Before it is too late. Look up to the Heavens, where God is, and seek for correct answers.

The Rights of the Unborn Child

Unborn children already possess God given inalienable rights guaranteed by our Constitution. No one should be able to take it away.

The US Supreme Court Justices should have known of these things, before they approved of allowing abortion as a legal right. With their faulty 5-4 decision they failed to protect the people they swore to protect.

And the big irony is: these Justices are considered as the best and highly educated citizens of the country, **BUT HAVE FAILED US**. What shall we do with these radical and renegade judges of our court systems? Shall we scrap them and find a new selection process. How can they be so deceived by the accuser, unbelievable! Shall we change our educational system too?

To my amazement: where was the religious community in that time; when the issue of Roe vs. Wade was being hotly debated; to articulate the rights of the defenseless unborn human beings, just for the rights of women? Why did they allow evil courts to corrupt what is God given?

Now I understand why the Bible say; man's intelligence is just foolishness to God. Bad things must not be happening to America. We are people who suppose to have great wisdom, because we live in an anointed nation. We should not fall prey to the accuser. Unfortunately, most of our leaders do. They are deceived **Big Time.**

So in choosing our leaders: we must be very careful. We must set our emotions aside. First thing first: choose a leader with moral integrity, a leader who knows how to pray. Divine blessings will come to the nation. If the President of the USA is a man of God, the country will prosper and will be at peace and less troubles overseas. Mark my word.

Women do not posses the right to abort life either, as well as the government.

Pro-choice abortion rights; is not included in the Free Will package given by God to man: It is an issue that cannot and should not exist in this world; for it is a mirage, it only seems to be a legitimate right. Not true at all. So don't be deceived.

First of all, we do not own our body and spirit. It belongs to the Creator God. The baby is not ours either, it belongs to the Creator too. God is using us as means to procreate, take good care of these babies until they grow up as young adults in the knowledge of the Word of God to serve His purpose.

There is a reason why this issue of the Gosnell trial is on Fox News lately, April 2014. I believe God wants us to take action and repeal Roe vs. Wade law. The time to start is now.

My first Solution is to Slow Down the Rate of Abortion for the meantime:

A portion of the sale of this book will be earmarked for the creation of a Foundation especially designed to provide: a) Counseling of young mothers against abortion, b) creation of orphanages around the world, c) education up to college degree for orphans, d) knowledge of the Word of God and e) repeal, Roe vs. Wade.

I urge my fellow Americans.
Take back the America we used to know.

Rom. 12:19 *Dearly beloved, avenge not yourselves, but rather give place unto wrath: for it is written, Vengeance is mine; I will repay, saith the Lord.* On behalf of the aborted babies, the Lord will repay as promised. Now to the abortionist: Wait until God comes your way, for I am certain that you will be punished accordingly. And you might not have the chance to repent. Regret is of no effect. It will be too late. The time to STOP the carnage of innocent babies is NOW. Take heed. My plea is no joke.

My plea goes to all who espouses abortion: I mean to all. These includes Supreme Court judges, pro choice supporters, women who believes that it is a God given right to abort because it is their own body, corporate people who are in the business of abortion, doctors and nurses who work in abortion clinics. All of you are guilty of murder of unborn babies. Don't wait for the vengeance of God to be on you, because it will not be pretty. Stop now and repent, while you still have time.

If you repent God will spare you from His wrath, His vengeance will be on the Evil spirits that deceived you that it is good to murder defenseless unborn babies.

CHAPTER 28

God REWARDS

Our God is a very Good God for He Rewards us for our obedience in doing His Will and Acceptance of God Given Righteousness.

God is rewarding us mightily for obeying and doing His will. And if we do His will, He calls it as we bear fruit. **If we bear fruit, we glorify His Name. If we glorify God's name, God will sanctify our spirit and body. Then we can enter the Kingdom of God.** Material blessings keeps flowing in as well.

Psalm 37:3 *Trust in the Lord and do good, so shall you dwell in the land, and verily you shall be fed.* Only put your trust in God and God alone and blessings will come flowing like milk and honey. **Psalm 23:1**. 100 fold blessings. No other Lord.

Psalm 37:4 *Delight yourself also in the Lord, and He shall give you the desires of your heart.* Only God can make these Promises. All we have to do is Trust and Believe. It is so simple.

Psalm 37:5 *Commit your way unto the Lord; trust also in Him; and He shall bring it to pass.* Even if we are in the midst of trials and tribulations and we see and feel that it is never ending, we must stay the course and our focus is on the prize of eternal life, for it is the only life that matters. Therefore fret not. As promised it will come to pass.

Psalm 37:6 *And He shall bring forth your righteousness as the light, and your judgment as the noonday.* Gives us our likeness to Christ.

Psalm 37:7 *Rest in the Lord, and wait patiently for Him: fret not because of him who prospers in his way, because of the man who brings wicked devices to pass.*

Psalm 37:9 *For evildoers shall be cutoff: but those who wait upon the Lord, they shall inherit the earth.*

These verses from **Ps. 37:3-9** gives us the four Keys to victory in life:

1) Trust, 2) Delight, 3) Commit, and 4) Rest. Use these four Keys day in and day out. And before we notice it, the desires of our heart have all come to pass. Also for us who waits: these 4 Keys will give us **Membership into the Body of Christ.**

Notes:

Victory in life means Christ dwells in us and we dwell in Him for we are **Members of the Body of Christ.**

Spiritual Wellness is the greatest thing all men must desire. It guarantees eternal life.

CHAPTER **29**

Where Will Our Spirits Go?

After Death

We now know that it is appointed unto man once to die. The reason is our corrupted body (because of sin) has to be separated from our soul and spirit. The body or flesh and bones are left to rot on the ground. God has no use of it, so it is not worth saving, because it bears the seed of Satan. God wants no part of it in any manner or form. Only the Spirit of Man is worth saving for it is the real man created in God's image. God can give us a new glorified body without any trace of corruption.

For the Spirit of the Redeemed:

The Church or follower of Christ: Our spirit will be consecrated, sanctified and will become **Members of the Body of Christ forever.** We are in Eternal Living with God, resting in peace, with no problems, sickness, sorrows, troubles and no pain and suffering. There is no condemnation or judgment.

At the Feast of the Great Atonement, Jesus Christ promised to give us back a **glorified body**. A body that is holy and perfect: a body that is the same as the body of Adam and Eve, when they are still without sin. They were not naked. Read the 8 Holy Days of God.

At Jesus Crucifixion: **Luke 23:42** *And he* (the thief) *said unto Jesus, Lord, remember me when You come into Your Kingdom.*

Luke 23: 43 *And Jesus said unto him. Verily I say unto you.* ***Today shall you be with Me in Paradise.***

The exact Biblical answer to the question: **Paradise.**

In **Romans 12:1-8,** It says, Believers will become **Members of the Body of Christ**. The headquarters of the Body of Christ is in **Paradise**. The Church will stay in Paradise to wait for the 2nd Coming of Christ. After Armageddon is finished Christ and the Saints will bind Satan and sent him to the bottomless pit to tempt no more. Then the Tree of Knowledge of Good and Evil will also be no more. And then the Day of Atonement will take place.

The **Garden of Eden** is in Paradise. And the **Tree of Life** is still in the midst of the Garden. **Genesis 2:8,** If we die now, I do not believe we are going to 3rd Heaven yet as some Bible scholars would want us to believe. We will go to Paradise as a **Member of the Body of Christ.**

When the Feast of Tabernacle is celebrated after the Battle of Armageddon, the New Heaven or New Jerusalem comes down from Heaven. Then Christ's Millennial Kingdom will be established and the **Members of the Body of Christ** will rule and reign with Him.

John the Baptist preaching; **Matthew 3:2** *And saying, Repent you: for the **Kingdom of Heaven** is at hand.*

Luke 17:21 ... *for behold, the **Kingdom of God** is within you.* **Luke 17:22,** .... *The days will come, when you shall desire to see the days of the **Son of Man**, and you shall not see it.* In **Matthew 6:33,** All these terminologies (names) that are highlighted in bold refers to Jesus Christ. Now do the math.

The privileges in being a **Member of the Body of Christ**, there is no way Satan can still touch us or tempt us or destroy us anymore; we are **under His total protection.** Because Christ defeated Satan by His Finished Work at Calvary. **Gen. 3:15**

At this present time, human eyes cannot see Paradise. Yes, it is still on Earth. But it is in the holy spiritual realm. Men are in the mortal realm. In the **Kingdom of Christ**, man will see the real **Paradise** again. USA is almost a paradise. Now that you have an idea, let us work together not to destroy it. But rather, let us work to bring our nation back to GOD for us to experience life in Paradise. In the mortal realm or the world, we still find the Tree of Knowledge of Good and Evil. Satan is still in this world where he can still tempt and destroy us if we allow him, but we have the means to reject him and be away from his deadly influence. We have the Body of Christ to go for refuge.

God of the Living

Matt. 22:32 Jesus said: *I am the God of Abraham, and the God of Isaac and the God of Jacob? God is not the God of the dead, but of the living.* The souls and spirit of the redeemed past and present are all alive and well. For God is with us. We are **Members of the Body of Christ.**

Now, the Spirit of the Unredeemed: Those who did not received Christ

His spirit and soul remains on the surface of the Earth, roaming around like zombies with no direction, waiting for the Great White Throne Judgment. The human spirit will be under horrible pain and suffering, there is no rest for them. Since the spirit cannot die, the suffering is eternal. Imagine if it is your spirit suffering for 2 to 3 more millenniums waiting for Judgment? Uhm! Ouch!

While waiting for the Great White Throne Judgment at the end of Christ Millennial Kingdom; the spirit and soul is free game for fallen angels, who are mean. He is subject to suffering, taunting, bullying and pain inflicted by the demons of Satan. Aside from the feeling of hunger, for they still have the desire to eat cooked food by living humans (but they will prefer not to touch foods that are not freely offered), they will feel the heat of day and the cold of the night as torment. For now that they are considered as graven spirits, they must hide beneath the earth. Plus the occasional strikes of lightning, that will throw them away into far unchartered territories. On the way back to their appointed places, they will encounter more torture.

The unredeemed Spirit has no power and strength to fight back or power to protect or to save itself. He is totally on his own. There is no one to protect them. **Now, anyone of you would still be willing to be subjected to this type of torture? And stay unredeemed. I hope and pray none.**

Those who will be possessed by demons, I believe they will end up in the Lake of Fire. Why? Because again; they will reject Christ Jesus for the second time, even at the Great White Throne Judgment.

I believe those who committed graver sin like murder will be in Hades. Where is Hades or Hell? As described by the Scriptures: it is a compartment deep down into the center of the Earth. There is a place of comfort and of torment, for there is a flame. Read **Luke 16:23-31.** I believe Hell and Lake of Fire are not the same place. Before Christ was resurrected Hades has two compartments: Paradise and Hell.

After Christ was crucified, He went down to Hades to claim His Old Testament Saints and when He was resurrected, He took with Him Paradise out of Hades and all the Saints (in Abraham's bosom) were also resurrected with Him. Today Hades has only one compartment: Hell.

To whosoever, that has the privilege to read this book? My question: Do you still want to continue to reject or oppose God?

Now, that you have this information? What are you going to do about it? It is my hope and prayers that wisdom is with you to do the right choice.

That is why our Lord Christ wants to save all now that no one shall perish, if only all would repent and accept Him as the Son of God. Jesus offered us the free gift of Grace: His finished Work on the Cross. With Him hanging on the cross is the means.

I don't believe a Pastor who said Jesus was not trying to save all. **Jesus can't save all because some rejects Him. The Bible says All, no exceptions.** To repeat: **Matt. 3:2.** *And saying, Repent you: for the Kingdom of Heaven is at hand.*

Matt. 3:11 *I indeed baptize, you with water unto Repentance: but He who comes after me is mightier than I, whose shoes I am not worthy to bear: He shall baptize you with Holy Spirit, and with fire.*

Baptism of the Holy Spirit started at the Feast of Pentecost, and continuously by Fire while we are still alive. That means trials and tribulations are normal. We should express our gratitude to our Father that we are being refined.

Again, the only solution to All of Our Problems is Jesus Christ:

We must trust in Him. If He can transform the water into a very excellent wine, raised Lazarus from the dead and be alive again, made Sarah, the wife of Abraham fertile, heal the lepers and make the blind see. He can also do the same for all of us. He can transform us to be Spiritually and be Physically alive. If we allow Christ to transform us we become **Members of the Body of Christ.** With God, nothing is impossible.

Chapter 30

Fathers

Eph 6:4 *And you fathers, provoke not your children to wrath, but bring them up in the nurture and admonition of the Lord.*

Fathers, if you are a **Member of the Body of Christ** you are the High Priest of your house, exercise these obligations that you have for your family. If you are not a member, you are not a High Priest, for you are coming empty handed. All fathers must secure this Priesthood. Without Christ we have nothing.

Learn the word of God and teach them, that they grow up with the right knowledge of the True God. For it is a delight in the eyes of God. You children will grow upright and surely the Lord will bless them.

I grew up in a household where the children kiss the hand of parents, Father first and the Mother second upon arriving home, either from school or work. And they will bless us in the Holy name of Christ. In reminiscing, I believe God has blessed me, and my family. Especially my children, that they attained success: that as a parent had never dreamed of. As a father, I give thanks to my

Father in Heaven, as well as I give thanks to my father on earth and my father in law.

When we get closer to our Most High God on a consistent basis, as fathers we must give our children a little advice here and there and teach them the Word of God here and there. Our children will emulate us more on how parents live or conduct our behavior at home and in business.

My advice to my fellow fathers; is be cognizant and observe the things that are happening to your children, inch by inch as they grow. You will note that slowly they begin to respond and they become more responsible and accountable to their own actions. Positive things are starting to pile up as good credits to your children. Good children make parents proud.

Parents: fathers be patient, just love your children no matter what. Give them space to grow. Don't ever let go of them especially if they get into trouble. Every day don't forget to bless them as they leave the house and as they come in. **They must receive blessings from you** (husband, father it is your privilege) **as the High Priest of the home.** Also don't forget to bless the mother of your children, in the same manner as God has anointed Abraham.

When a Father blesses his children, the blessing goes a long way. The scripture says the blessing reaches up to 4 generations. Your blessings will keep your seed off, of the poor house. Our society will have few of our population on skid row and in prison. America will be much more greater than we are now.

Therefore I say unto my fellow parents: Never curse your children even if your anger reaches the heavens. Always forgive them once you are finished with your admonitions. Why am I saying this? I have family experience like this scenario with my uncle. And it was ugly for I have seen how much my cousins, nieces and nephews have suffered because of the family curse. My uncle quarreled with my grandfather and at his deathbed, my grandpa asked my uncle to come so he can be forgiven, but my uncle hardened his heart and did not. I saw how my uncles' seeds miss the blessings of God. For whatever they do, it seems they were not bearing any good fruit. I pray that all may understand this and no one will ever go through it.

The Bible says curses also affects up to 4 generations. But curses can be broken, if someone in the family finds its way to Christ to salvation. A member of the family, who is saved, must pray and call all who are affected by their names. Pray that our Father in Heaven will call them to become followers of Christ. (Remember the story of how Christ raised Lazarus from the dead.)

Fathers, it is our duty to pray incessantly for the welfare of our children, so that they will be blessed: by our Father in Heaven. And that: all of them may be called to be **Members of the Body of Christ.**

CHAPTER 31

Faith and Works

James 2:20 *But will you know, O vain man, that Faith without works is dead?*

Yes, we do believe in one God, but when our Faith is so little, that we will not follow it up with works, we should know when God ask us to do something usually it is something that will glorify the Lord. Just like Jonah, we run away from God. For sure, God will ask us for something to work on. God will tell us through dreams, visions and listening to His still small voice. As **Member of the Body of Christ,** each one of us has different function and purpose. And these functions must be performed and purpose fulfilled. If we don't do what is supposed to be done, then our faith is dead. This is one reason why a believer is cut off from the True Vine. We don't want that to happen to us.

James 2:21 *Was not Abraham our father Justified by works, when he had to offer Isaac his son upon the Altar?* Of course, not every one of us will be asked to offer one of our sons upon the Altar? I believe the most common work is to help fulfill Christ Great Commission: to help bring the Gospel of Christ up to the ends of the Earth. How? Obviously by giving tithes and love offering to your local Church or congregations and ministries. We have to present our bodies as a Living sacrifice holy and perfect.

There are many more gifts will be given to us that we can work on, and we must ask the Holy Spirit for guidance on what to do. He will tell us exactly what will be our function or purpose as a member. Look to interpret your dreams, visions and revelations that are given by God. Most importantly, listen to His still small voice. These are the ways, how He communicates with His children. To accomplish and fulfill God's Will is very important, as it is our defining moment. The Bible says: God will bless us more by the fruit we bear.

Each one of us, who are **Members of the Body of Christ** is blessed and anointed. We receive revelations from the Father through Jesus, and each revelation is different from one another. In Bible study classes, I have to be cognizant of things around me, as we tackle to understand each verse, each one will have a different take on the topic, some shallow, some very profound understanding and some presents very interesting view. There is no right and wrong. When these things happen, I say wow! I am amazed. Then I know that Christ is amongst us. **Luke 17:21**

God's will and revelation for me is; I believe is writing this book to tell the whole world: Who is Santo Nino de Cebu? Who is Santo Nino de Atocha? Who is the Holy Child of Prague? What, or who is the Body of Christ.

Is this Christ's preparation for His second advent?

James 2:22 *Seest thou how Faith wrought with his works, and by works was Faith made perfect?* Look at happened to Abraham, our father in Faith. He was justified by his Faith and was validated by his works. That he has loyalty and because he did what he has to do with Isaac, God blessed him mightily. God said in blessing, I will bless you and in multiplying I will multiply you. . . Apostle Paul said: We are justified by Faith in Christ Jesus only, and that faith was made perfect by good works. Therefore Faith and Works goes hand in hand. They are inseparable. There should be no debate.

James 2:23 *And the scripture was fulfilled which said, Abraham believed God, and it was imputed unto him for Righteousness*

James 2:24 *You see how that by works a man is Justified, and not by Faith only.* As a child of God, the Holy Spirit will talk to us in so many ways: in dreams, vision, events in our lives, or His small still voice, and He will give us assignments to work on. **If we can discern God's messages to us and do His will, then our Faith will be made perfect unto good works. We glorified the entire Godhead.**

Christ Jesus loved us first, it is just right to return His love by loving one another. For if we love all our neighbors, we already shown that we love Jesus.

Our works validates how great is our faith in Our Father in Heaven.

The Eight (8) Holy Days of God (Old Testament)

Day of Passover	A lamb sacrificed and blood placed on doors of Israelite houses in Egypt and God "passed over" Lev. 23:5	April 14, 2014 April 3, 2015 April 22, 2016 April 10, 2017 March 30, 2018
Feast of Unleavened Bread, + First Fruits	A 7 day Feast where unleavened bread is only eaten. No leaven is allowed. Lev. 23:6-14	April 15-21, 2014 April 4-10, 2015 April 23-29, 2016 April 11-17, 2017 Mar 31-Apr6, 2018
Feast of Pentecost	A 1 day, celebrating the gathering of first smaller annual harvest. 50 days after Passover. Lev. 23:15-22	June 8, 2014 May 24, 2015 June 12, 2016 June 4, 2017 May 20, 2018
Feast of Trumpets	Called Rosh Hashana, A day of rejoicing marked by blowing of Trumpets Lev. 23:23-25	Sept. 25, 2014 Sept. 14, 2015 October 3, 2016 Sept. 21, 2017 Sept. 10, 2018

Day of Atonement	Called Yom Kippur, A day of fasting and Repentance. Lev. 23:26-32	October 4, 2014 Sept. 23, 2015 October 12, 2016 Sept. 30, 2017 Sept 19, 2018
Feast of Tabernacles	A 7 day Feast of the great fall harvest. Observed by living in booths looking up. Lev. 23:33-43	October 9-15, 2014 Sep. 28-Oct 4, 2015 Oct. 17-23, 2016 Oct. 5-11, 2017 Sept. 24-30, 2018
Feast of Last Great Day	A Monday after the Feast of Tabernacles. The eight day. A separate Feast. Lev. 23:36-39	October 16, 2014 October 5, 2015 October 24, 2016 October 12, 2017 October 1, 2018

The Eight Holy Days of God (New Testament)

Day of Passover (Prophecy Fulfilled) Mark 15:33-41, Matt. 27:45-56	Jesus Christ as the sacrificial Lamb, shedding His blood for the sins of Mankind. Man has to accept God's gift of Grace.
Feast of Unleavened Bread + First Fruits (Prophecy Fulfilled) Matt. 28:1-7, Luke 24:1-8	Those who, accepts Christ as Lord and Savior to put out their sins from a life yielding to walk with Jesus. The Resurrection.

Day of Pentecost (Prophecy Fulfilled) Acts 2:1-13, 17	The Holy Spirit coming down from Heaven to dwell among believers. The Body of Christ is being gathered.
Feast of the Trumpets 1 Thess. 4:13-18	Starts with the Rupture of the Saints. Pictures a time of war, plagues (tribulation) concluding with the 2nd Coming of Christ.
Day of Atonement Rev. 20:4, 6	Pictures the Sanctification of the Saints and binding of Satan at the end of the Battle of Armageddon.
Feast of Tabernacles Rev.21:1-11, 22:1	Pictures the coming down of New Heaven or New Jerusalem, with Saints looking up and expectant.
Feast of Last Great Day Rev. 19:9-10, 22:17	Pictures the Great Wedding. Jesus Christ the Bridegroom and His Church as the Bride.

Fig. 1 – The Tree of Life, an Illustration only
Symbolic of the Body of Christ and the True Vine

The Tree of Life or the Body of Christ: Picture the Following:

1. **The Ground or the Lump**: is the Earth, is the 3rd Rock from the Sun, is the Jehovah Jireh, is the Father God; is the Vinedresser or Husbandman. John 15:1-7

2. **The Roots**: is the Jewish Roots – Abraham, Isaac, and Jacob; King David; and King Solomon; and all of Jesus genealogy from Abraham to Joseph, husband of Mary. Matt. 1:1-17

3. **The Trunk or Stem**: is Jesus Christ, is the True Vine, is the vertical part of the Cross; is the Body; is the Shepherd; is the Emanuel; is the King of Kings; is our Counselor; is our Comforter; is our Savior; is our Deliverer; is the Warrior against Evil; is the Holy Spirit; the Living Water; the Bread of Life; the Kingdom of God; the Kingdom of Heaven; Paradise; our Treasure. Matt. 6:33, Luke 17:21,

4. **The Branches:** is the Church; is the Sheep; is the Believer; is considered a Cell or a Family or Members of the Body of Christ; the horizontal part of the Cross. John 15:2-4

5. **The Fruits:** is God's rewards to His Church's Good Works; is the Treasures stored in Heaven; is the Fruit of the Womb; is the gift of Grace: Faith, Hope and Love; is God's provision of the Daily Bread; is the Manna.

For obeying His commandments and doing God's will, man is sanctified and shall live forever.

Notes:

Warning:

To people around the World who have accepted Jesus Christ as their Lord and Saviour: Congratulations, you are a Member of the Body of Christ. You have received God's free gift of grace and eternal Life.

To people of this World who continues to reject and oppose the Word of God: My condolences for you are spiritually dead, until such time in the future that you come to your senses and accept Christ as your Lord and Saviour. The best time to accept Jesus is now. For your tomorrow may never come. Or else you are destined to the Lake of Fire. Remember to visualize: the Lake of Fire can be similar to the Sun, eternal hot place.

Jesus said: *I am the Way, the Truth and the Life.*

Doxology:

Jude 24. *Now unto Him who is able to keep you from falling, and to present you faultless before the Presence of His Glory with exceeding joy.*

Jude 25. *To the only wise God our Saviour, be Glory and Majesty, Dominion and Power, both now and Forever. Amen.*

As **Members of the Body of Christ,** we give a heartfelt thanks to our Lord Jesus Christ, for His finished work at the Cross made this Benediction all possible

Purpose for Writing this Book:

To spearhead a fund raising movement on behalf of Santo Nino Chapel of Aromin: A revelation came to the congregation about 3 years ago that Santo Nino or the Body of Christ wants to build a big Church building next to the chapel. A place of worship: where devotees in the region can congregate and express their Faith to Our Father in Heaven.

The Santo Nino Chapel of Aromin, Echague, Isabella
Address: Barangay Aromin – Purok 3,
Echague, Isabela, Philippines
Curators:
Mr. & Mrs. Renato & Estrella Ramones
Phil. Contact Mobile #s: 0919-765-1728.
0921-268-5691,
USA, Magic Jack: 15624158486 or 15622367333
www.membersboc.com
email: samaritanhp@yahoo.com

Activities at this facility:
Mass or prayer group every Sunday
and Free Spiritual Healing 24/7.

The Free Spiritual healing has become a health lifeline for the surrounding community as most of the citizens are poor farmers. She will accept donation, whatever amount the patient can donate and will not put a price on her work.

On several occasions in the last 2 years, the Image of Santo Nino has revealed to the congregation of His intention to build a big place of worship beside the chapel, so that almost all of the believers in the whole region will have a place to worship the Father.

The proceeds will be used solely for Real Property acquisition, church building, office building, roads and other support facilities.

Approximate size of the proposed church building is 112-144 meters diameter and 12 meters high and the tower is about 5 meters high above the building. These are just initial estimates. The approximate cost is about P3B to 4B or $ 75M to $ 100M.

We hope to start building in 2-3 years. Count up from June 2014.

For additional photos of the Chapel: **facebook/ catlea ramones/** album.

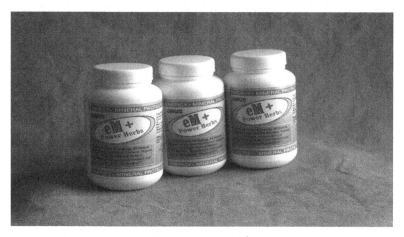

eM+ Power Herbs

A superb Anti-Oxidant. The action of this Dietary
Supplement is discussed in this Book. This is the
supplement that best counters the evil works of
Satan as Prince of the Power of the Air.
Medical efficacy by Cellular Polarization or Cellular Balance.
Contains 400 to 1000 meq/100 grams of negatively charged
ions. The mineral negative ions that neutralizes oxidants.
www.Z88-88ph.com
email: samaritanhp@yahoo.com
Please place your donation and orders online or by email, or
best, call us first: In the USA # 15624158486; or 15622367333
For clients in the Phil, please call: 09212685691.
Expected Donation is $ 50.00. Free Shipping
Book, the Body of Christ - $ 25.00, and
eM+ Power Herbs- $ 25.00/bottle.

REFERENCES:

1. King James Version of the Holy Bible, KJV
2. The Expositors Study Bible, by Jimmy Swaggart Ministries
3. New International Version of the Holy Bible, NIV
4. Tomorrow's World Magazine, Issue July – August 2012
5. The Week Magazine, April 26, 2013 issue
6. Unveiling Ancient Biblical Secrets, by Larry Huch Ministries
7. Wikipedia.com (Santo Nino)
8. The Klassen Calendarized Study Bible, KJV

SIDE NOTES:

- The God of Abraham, Isaac and Jacob is a **Capitalist**: Capitalism is not synonymous with Materialism by any stretch of anyone's imagination. But the left and the communists are twisting and exploiting the young college students and the low information people to believe the lie. Unfortunately, the educated and the so-called progressive groups are also buying into the deception posted by those who are greedy to profit from this. Whoever is or are funding Occupy Wall Street Movement are guilty to be one of these greedy groups. Unfortunately, also the conservatives and the religious community do not know how to articulate and defend their core beliefs.

- **On American Obesity Problem.** The people, who are worried and wanted to solve this problem are barking at the wrong tree for solutions. I believe someone in the medical industry already knows the answer and are keeping quiet and are looking for ways to profit more from the problem. I believe I have the answers. Sadly I have to put a few big industries out of business. The Soda, soft drink industry is the cause of obesity. It takes at least 2 generation for it to be noticed.

- **On Smoking** – I agree that smoking cigarettes is bad enough for any closed environment. But the government exploited the problem by tagging its supposedly adverse medical effects on the lungs. The truth is it is a scam. The true cause of lung cancer is not from smoking. Probably they did not know it. The government profited from the huge taxes levied on the smoking public. My other concern is the California anti-smoking TV ads are flawed and deceptive. Perhaps it is a blessing in disguise as no smoker profits from it anyway. Still I don't buy the deception, for deception is of evil.

- **Cannabis** – The true noble use for this flowering plant has not been discovered yet. But the unhealthy use has been. Now the people who wants to smoke was handed by our enemy a way to get around anti smoking Laws. What the government and most people don't know is that smoking cannabis is much worse than smoking tobacco. Marijuana kills the brains of the user. And users are becoming useless people because most would not want to work, instead just lay down in all day. It is a downer. The argument for its medical use is only a façade, a deception. I don't buy it. American voters bought another lie. Adverse effects will be endured sooner than we are told. Then we regret.

Capitalism

Capitalism is not materialism. As the socialist and communist (the left and the progressives) wants you to believe. For they love to twist and exploit the facts from God. When I see this, I know Satan is at work.

Capitalism is God's way of creating wealth. When we work with God as our partner, we succeed and produce wealth so that no one should be poor. The creation of wealth is exponential. Similar to the 5 loaves of bread and 2 fishes miracle. Multiplied by Jesus to feed up to 25000 people. Read **Matt. 25:14-30** the Parable of Talents, where God encourages us to produce wealth from the blessings He has given to whom He wants to give. Because in the wealth we produce we should share to our brothers. If sharing the wealth takes place no one should be poor. By sharing, we glorify our Father in Heaven.

Whereas: materialism is the love of money (root of all evil), the hoarding of wealth for personal gain and taking advantage of others. This is corruption, and it is the reason why so many are poor. So many businessmen and entrepreneurs have been riding on the backs of common working people who were gravely underpaid. They don't know how to bless others with their blessings. This is

Romito S. Olaguer

common especially in the retail business. Just watch and know who is who. The rich has an obligation to share his riches to the poor by way of work employment with more than enough wages. Not by doling out money to look good in the eyes of people.

Therefore don't confuse yourself of these two terminologies. This is how our young college graduates have been taught that Capitalism is bad. They don't know that materialism is greed and evil. Pathetic. In Rev. 18, the Scriptures say: that Jesus Christ will destroy the new Babylon or the world of materialism.

Why is there so much gap between the rich and the poor in this world? Simply because; the rich forgot about the poor. They forgot their obligation to share the wealth they were entrusted to manage and be good steward of God's wealth. This is the job of Christian Church to lead to establish a system of equitable distribution of wealth around the world.

The leading country with religious charitable institution or foundation in the world is the United States of America. Still it is too little to make a considerable impact on alleviating poverty around the world. We also need a comprehensive corporate involvement where the manufacturing of goods should not be concentrated in one country alone. It has to be equitably distributed as well to many poor 3rd world countries. At this moment it is concentrated in China. Why not develop Africa and South America?

If only all can believe and accept Jesus Christ then we obtain Spiritual Wellness: that is Eternal Life, all we need to do is to become a Member of the Body of Christ so that we become a permanent resident/citizen in Paradise. For all we did on Earth, this is our crowning glory to be with our maker again. There is no greater achievement that we must aspire for. This is it, folks!

God Bless to all **Members of the Body of Christ.**